cycling **traffic-free**
LONDON

Ian Allan
PUBLISHING

Cycling Traffic-Free; London
Jules Selmes

First published 2011

ISBN 978 07110 3525 6

Published by Ian Allan Publishing

An imprint of Ian Allan Publishing Ltd, Hersham, Surrey KT12 4RG.
Printed in England by Ian Allan Printing Ltd, Hersham, Surrey KT12 4RG.

Visit the Ian Allan Publishing website at www.ianallanpublishing.com

Distributed in the United States of America and Canada by BookMasters Distribution Services.

Code 1104/D3

CONTENTS

THE MAIN ROUTES

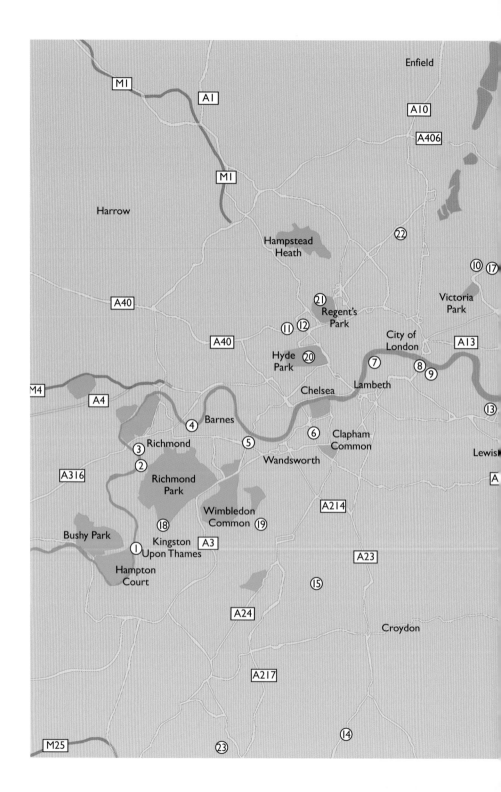

Enfield

M1

A1

A10

A406

M1

Harrow

Hampstead
Heath

㉒

⑩ ⑰

A40

㉑

Regent's
Park

Victoria
Park

⑪ ⑫

City of
London

A13

A40

Hyde
Park

⑳

⑦

⑧
⑨

Chelsea

Lambeth

M4

A4

⑬

Barnes

④

⑥

Clapham
Common

Lewis

Richmond

⑤

③

Wandsworth

②

A

A316

Richmond
Park

Wimbledon
Common

⑲

A214

Bushy Park

⑱

Kingston

A3

①
Upon Thames

A23

Hampton
Court

⑮

A24

Croydon

A217

M25

㉓

⑭

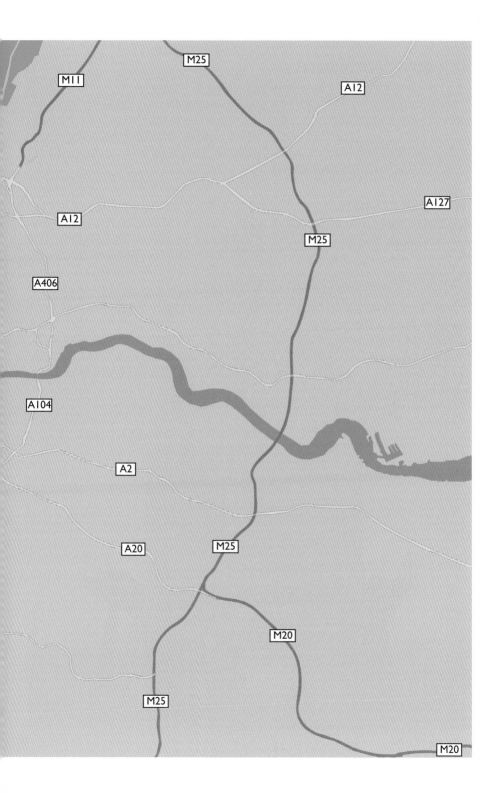

ACKNOWLEDGEMENTS

This book would not have been possible without the help and support of my wife, Linda. Thanks also to Wilf Davis for accompanying me on a few of the rides; his good humour and patience were essential. I must also thank the many cyclists who allowed me to photograph them as they cycled past – especially those who agreed to do it several times! They all acknowledged the need for a guide such as this, and I hope they will not be disappointed.

INTRODUCTION

There has never been a better time to enjoy cycling in London. In the last ten years there has been a marked increase in the number of areas accessible to cyclists, and also better provision on the roads. This is due in part to the tireless campaigning of Sustrans and the London Cycle Campaign, but also to the Government's realisation that promoting cycling can lead to fewer cars on the road and a general improvement in the public health. Exploring London by bicycle will reveal a great deal of its history and heritage, as well as its natural beauty (and, if you are lucky, some of its wildlife too).

I would recommend that readers familiarise themselves with their chosen route first, using this book and a Transport for London map. This guide differs from the others in this series in that seldom is the rider anywhere really remote, or far from food, drink, provisions and toilet facilities.

The routes in this book will take you alongside rivers and canals, roads and railways as well as across open countryside and through urban sprawl. Whether you are in a cycle lane on a road or a sandy path next to a river, the perceptive cyclist will be able to enjoy the many different environments. Although the aim of this book is to provide traffic-free rides, you will unavoidably encounter urban traffic at times. This need not be intimidating or dangerous, as long as you use commonsense and follow a few basic rules:

- Ride in a confident and predictable manner. Do not run red lights or ride up one-way streets the wrong way.
- Use clear hand signals when changing direction. Car drivers will be less likely to get irritated by a slow-moving bike and make thoughtlessly aggressive manoeuvres.
- Do not cycle in the gutter, where the sudden need to avoid broken glass, dog's mess or general debris can lead to accidents. Being that bit further out into the road gives you more room to manoeuvre and means cars will have to take you into consideration when passing.
- Remember that car drivers do not benefit from the cyclist's wider/higher field of vision. Lorries and vans have blind spots too.
- Try to read the traffic and recognise dangerous situations before they develop. Sometimes it may be better to wave a car ahead, or let it out of a side street and out of your way, rather than getting into a tussle for supremacy on the road!
- Make eye contact with drivers and smile. Your interaction with drivers will influence how they approach the next cyclist they cross paths with.

THE CYCLIST'S CODES
The Highway Code
Know the laws of the road: rules 59-82 were written specifically for cyclists, so take time to read them. If you hold a British driving licence and then commit a misdemeanour (e.g. riding drunk) while on your bicycle, you are liable to have points imposed on your licence (www.direct.gov.uk/en/TravelAndTransport/Highwaycode/index.htm).

The Countryside Code
Reviewed and renamed in 2004, this was originated by the National Parks Commission in 1951, when it was known as the Country Code, and integrated into the Highway Code later in the 1950s. It mostly consists of commonsense and good manners:
- Be safe – plan ahead and follow any signs.
- Leave gates and property as you find them.
- Protect plants and animals, and take your litter home.
- Keep dogs under close control.
- Consider other people.

(These five rules are expanded upon at the Natural England website: http://www.naturalengland.org.uk)

The Waterways Code
Considerate cycling is permitted by British Waterways, providing this code of conduct is followed:

- 'Pass people slowly. Give people space. Pedestrians have priority over cyclists on the towpath. Slow down when approaching pedestrians and only pass when it is safe to do so. Extra care should be taken when passing children, less able people and animals. Try to pass on the waterside of the path. Pedestrians will tend to move to the back edge of the towpath to allow you to pass. Be patient and courteous toward pedestrians. Saying "thank you" to pedestrians who move to let you pass will make them more likely to move next time.'
- 'Ring with **Two Tings**.' This is not an order to pedestrians to get out of your

way. 'Be aware that some people might have visual or hearing impairments and may not hear your **Two Tings**.'

- 'Be extra careful at bends and entrances. Cyclists should be prepared to slow down, stop or dismount, if necessary.'
- 'Give way to oncoming users at bridges. Some bridges have poor visibility, so check (using the mirrors, if available) that someone isn't already coming through. Cyclists should slow down, ring with **Two Tings** and let other users through the bridge before continuing. Never pass a pedestrian or another cyclist underneath a bridge – there is not enough room to do so safely.' (Please note that cyclists are no longer expected to dismount in order to go under a bridge.)
- 'Consider other users and the local environment.' Watch out for anglers' tackle and give them time to move it if it is temporarily obstructing the path. Don't stray from the towpaths and take all litter home with you.
- 'Ride at a sensible speed for the towpath conditions. The towpath is never suitable for cycling fast as there are many other users, low bridges and narrow sections. If you are in a hurry, do not use the towpath, please use the road.'

Some stretches of the canal network can be remote and isolated, so they are better ridden with a companion; it is not advisable to ride these paths alone, especially if you are young or female. Check for any towpath closures on the British Waterways website (www.waterscape.com/things-to-do/boating/stoppages or www.twitter.com/TowpathRanger) before following any routes that include the canal network. When cycling within the Royal Parks, please be aware of where bicycles are not allowed (www.royalparks.org.uk).

ACCESS AND THE LAW

Access for cyclists is getting better all the time. Cycling is now allowed without a permit on British Waterways' canal and river paths throughout Greater London, and many local councils have permitted access to pathways adjacent to busy roads, next to rivers, across open land or through parkland. Please adhere to these permitted routes and respect any prohibitions that are in place.

Off-road cyclists have access to bridleways, byways open to all traffic (BOATs) and roads used as public paths (RUPPs). These routes are clearly shown on Ordnance Survey maps. Compared to the busy roads, the clearer pavements may look appealing, but don't be tempted to ride on them unless you see the shared pathway signs. Some of the routes in this book do include 'no cycling' sections in order to allow for a continuous route or to avoid dangerous traffic junctions, but it is illegal to cycle on these paths and you may be penalised if you do. So dismount and walk.

CYCLING WITH CHILDREN

There are few things more enjoyable than cycling along on a pleasant, sunny day with your young child strapped into their seat behind you. When they get older, you can point out things along the way. Before you know it, they will be on their own bikes – racing you up hills and beating you!

It is generally considered to be safe to take a child out in a bike seat once they can hold up their head (and their helmet) on their own. A good bike seat should offer padded head protection without hindering the child's view and have straps to keep them in place, especially when they fall asleep. Foot straps are also vital. Look out for a model that allows plenty of adjustment as your child grows. Bike trailers are also an option for the youngest children; it is recommended that the trailer be covered to prevent your back wheel flicking water, grit or dog mess into the child's face. A bike seat or trailer should be suitable until your child is about four, when they may progress to a tag-along trailer bike (which usually clamps onto your bike's seat post).

There are three routes in this book suited to younger riders with their families: Route 22 (the Parkland Walk and Finsbury Park), Route 18 (Richmond Park) and Route 25 (Epping Forest). There are also sections of other routes especially suited to young children, e.g. the 2.5 miles of cycling within Nonsuch Park (Route 23: Epsom Downs loop), the 1.75 miles within Battersea Park (Route 06: Battersea to Putney Bridge via Chelsea

Harbour) and just under 2 miles within Victoria Park (Route 17: River Lea Navigation). If you have older children, I highly recommend you ride the route without them first, to assess if they can cope with the sections where it is not possible to follow a traffic-free route.

CYCLING NGOs

There are three main non-governmental organisations of interest to cyclists who ride in London.

London Cycling Campaign (www.lcc.org.uk)

LCC has been campaigning tirelessly for years to make cycling in London safer and more enjoyable. Their membership includes a magazine, store discounts, third-party insurance and free legal advice if involved in an accident. They also promote cycling in the city with a number of events and workshops in a range of cycling-specific subjects, especially during National Bike Week. LCC also organise free social rides.

Sustrans (www.sustrans.org.uk)

The UK's leading transport charity, which organises, maintains and promotes the National Cycle Network (NCN). Their vision is of a world in which people choose to travel in ways that benefit their health and the environment. Sustrans' work has resulted in a number of cycle routes across London, parts of which appear in this guide. As a charity, they rely on donations and fundraising by supporters. Please consider donating after you have ridden on one of their NCN routes, which will allow you to appreciate how well-designed and how well signposted their routes are. They also offer an online route-mapping tool.

Cyclists' Touring Club (www.ctc.org.uk/)

CTC is the UK's national cyclists' organisation, protecting and promoting the rights of cyclists since 1878. It campaigns locally and nationally on issues important to cyclists, and as a non-profit making organisation is funded through its membership and donations. With around 60,000 members nationally, it encompasses all ages and types of cyclists with elected representation at national and local level, backed by a professional staff. CTC provides a wide range of activities and services designed to enhance riding opportunities and to make it easier for new cyclists to take up the activity. Membership includes £10m insurance covering damage or injury to a third party, cycling-related legal advice, a bi-monthly magazine, discounts on cycling products online and in local shops, online advice and information about routes and events.

Transport for London (TfL)

TfL is the government body that is responsible for the transport system within Greater London. Cycling has recently been part of its agenda. The TfL website also produces 14 free maps showing the best cycle routes within Greater London. TfL are also building 'cycle superhighways' to improve cycling conditions for people who already commute by bike and to encourage new cyclists. They are planning 12 arterial routes across London to help cyclists cross the capital on their way to traffic-free or low-traffic routes. Please report any street faults such as potholes, faulty traffic lights or damaged or missing signs online, at tfl.gov.uk, or phone 0845 305 1234.

TRAVELLING WITH YOUR BIKE

By Train

The train companies operating in and out of London have their own policies relating to bicycles, so it is advisable to check before attempting to travel. Generally, only folding cycles are allowed on trains during the morning and evening rush hours. The Docklands Light Railway (DLR) will only allow folding cycles that are in a bag. Cycles are allowed on some parts of the tube network, generally where services run overground, but not between 0730-0930 and 1600-1900. A map showing exactly where bicycles are permitted on the underground network is available on the TfL website. Only folding bikes are allowed on trams.

By Car

If driving to get to the beginning of a cycle route, remember to check and see if it is within the Congestion Charge Zone: a clearly defined zone of central London where, between the hours of 07:00 and 18:00, Monday to Friday, you have to pay a £10 tariff. Also consider the cost of parking and be very aware of any parking restrictions; London's traffic wardens and vehicle clampers can be ruthless. The website www.parkatmyhouse.co.uk offers an alternative way to find a day's parking, which is very convenient and cheaper than a parking ticket. The website www.en.parkopedia.co.uk offers the same service but also lists street parking, car parks and controlled parking zones. Make sure all valuables are locked out of sight in the boot of your car.

CYCLING TRAFFIC-FREE:
LONDON
THE MAIN ROUTES

ROUTE 1
Kingston to Teddington Lock via Hampton Court Palace

Distance: 14 miles.

Map: Ordnance Survey Explorer map 161 and TfL Local Cycling Guide 9.

Surface and Gradients: Flat all-weather tarmac roads and gravel river paths. Small parts of the route along the river north of Teddington Lock, known as Ham Lands, can be muddy in places when wet.

Roads and road crossings: Good routing and cycle provision for NCN 4 mean that the only hazard is from pedestrians ambling into the cycle lanes. In Teddington there is a short busy section from Park Road (A309) to High Street, and again on Ferry Road, but both can easily be walked.

Refreshments: There is a café at Hampton Court Palace that must be walked to. Adjacent to Hampton Court Bridge are a few restaurants. There are also a few pubs along the route: Anglers and Tide End Cottage (Teddington Lock), Royal Oak on Sandy Lane (Ham) and New Inn (Ham Common). This whole route falls within the London Borough of Richmond's community toilet scheme where shops, pubs and restaurants allow the public to use their toilets during normal business hours.

Entering the Round Plantation at Bushy Park.

The most westerly route in the book can be split into three sections. The first goes south from Kingston to Hampton Court Palace and into Bushy Park. The second follows Cobblers Walk before sweeping around to cross the Thames at Teddington Lock. The final section follows the Thames around Ham Land and Ham House before coming back to Teddington Lock.

BACKGROUND AND PLACES OF INTEREST
Hampton Court Palace
From its humble beginnings as a grange for the Knights Hospitallers in 1236, various monarchs have tried to stamp their mark on Hampton Court Palace. Henry VIII's developments in the Tudor period are probably the best known, so be sure to visit the Great Halls. The next major stage of development was initiated by King William III and Queen Mary II when they came to power and commissioned Sir Christopher Wren to rebuild the palace. The gardens will not disappoint either, set over 60 acres. The famous maze was originally planted in 1690 as an amusement for William III.

Bushy Park
The name is thought to have originated from thorny bushes planted to protect young oak trees grown to provide timber for the Navy. The Chestnut Avenue was started as an avenue of limes in 1622. When Wren redesigned Hampton Court, it was extended and chestnut trees were planted. At this time a road was also built across Bushy Park leading to the Lion Gate at Hampton Court. In 1713, a statue of the nymph Arethusa and a fountain (the Diana Fountain) were placed in a basin in the middle of Wren's grand avenue.

Starting Points & Parking
1. Kingston – via South West Trains' Waterloo-Shepperton line, and also on a loop to Waterloo that includes Strawberry Hill, Twickenham, Wimbledon and Clapham Junction. Kingston has controlled parking zones, but there are also numerous car parks. One of the best placed is on Thameside.
2. Teddington – via the same points of access as Kingston, above.

Links to Other Routes
Route 02 – Ham Common to Richmond Lock Loop.
Route 18 – Richmond Park (via Ham Gate Avenue, off Ham Common).

ROUTE INSTRUCTIONS

1. Exit Kingston station, turn right and walk for 60 metres past a lay-by. Begin cycling, taking the shared path (signposted 'London Network 4') to the right which leads over the underpass. At the traffic lights, turn left across Wood Street using the cycle crossing and continue along the green cycle lane. This is NCN 4 and is well signposted. Follow the road to the right onto Clarence Street. Take the cycle lane to the left to cross Kingston Bridge.

2. Take the first left onto Barge Walk. Stay on the tarmac road until it runs out (at the barrier across the road) before joining the riverside path, to avoid anglers and pedestrians. The track is yellow/brown gravel for a further 1.65 miles, before changing back to tarmac.

3. The wrought iron screens of the Palace are on the right. To cut off the busy Hampton Court Road, dismount and walk through the palace gardens via the gate off the riverside path. Walk north across the front of the palace towards Lion Gate and enter Bushy Park using the zebra crossing.

4. Continue up to Hampton Court Bridge and Hampton Court Way (A309). Leave NCN 4 at this point. Dismount and use the pedestrian crossing on the right to turn and cross the A309. Confident riders can cycle straight ahead over the roundabout, staying on Hampton Court Road which bends to the right. (Less confident riders should walk past the roundabout before resuming.) Turn left into Bushy Park through Hampton Court Gate, just before the Liongate Hotel.

5. (a) If the traffic is not heavy, make a circuit around the Diana Fountain. Heading back towards Hampton Court Gate, turn off the road onto a sealed path. (b) Otherwise, after a short distance, cross over to the right where you see yellow cross hatching on the road and take the gravel path through the oak trees. Turn

Wrought iron screens at Hampton Court, created by Jean Tijou.

right where it joins the sealed path, passing a playground after which the path is unsealed.

6. Continue straight ahead for 900 metres before taking the left hand fork around a cricket pitch and up to Hampton Wick Gate. For an early end to the route, take the right fork up Church Grove Passage and then left at the T-junction onto Hampton Court Road (B308). It may be better to use the zebra crossing to cross before the roundabout to travel back over Kingston Bridge before retracing the route back to the station.

7. Turn left where the path forks at a sealed path and join Cobblers Walk. Pass the Leg of Mutton Pond on the left and the Warren Plantation on the right to carefully cross Chestnut Avenue. Carry straight onto a gravel path which leads onto the road. Keep left at the fork in the road, leaving Cobblers Walk to follow the line of trees. Take care passing the entrance/exit of the Pheasantry Welcome Centre, following the road for a while before the track becomes unsealed. Take the right-hand fork, cross Ash Walk and carry on following the trees. The track returns to a sealed road next to a house and passes an avenue of chestnut trees on the right.

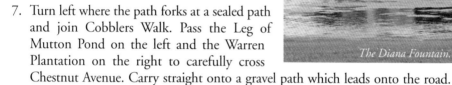
The Diana Fountain.

8. Turn right by the gate for Dukes Head Passage, away from the trees into the open parkland. Go straight on at the crossroads with Upper Lodge Road, passing cricket pitches on each side of the track to exit Bushy Park at Coleshill Road Gate.

9. Pass the back of the National Physical Laboratory to continue onto Coleshill Road. Turn right onto Queen's Road and first left up Park Lane.

10. (a) To finish at Teddington station, turn right onto Park Road and take the first left up Adelaide Road. (b) To continue the route, turn left onto Park Road. (Less confident riders should walk for the next 250 metres.) Cycle uphill taking the right-hand lane to turn right at the roundabout onto High Street.

11. Take the second left into Elmfield Avenue. Turn right at the T-junction into Cambridge Road then first left into Manor Road, which bends right into Twickenham Road.

12. Turn left onto Ferry Road. Go straight on at the traffic lights, down to the river. Take the footbridges over the Thames at Teddington Lock.

13. Turn left at the bottom of the ramp towards the lock. If the river is very high the path adjacent to Ham House may be flooded, so turn right here to return to Kingston. The route is quite densely wooded for the 1.5 miles to Ham House, obscuring the view of the river.

14. The path emerges from the trees. Just after the car park at Hammerton's Ferry, turn right away from the river along a boardwalk. Turn right and join the road that runs in front of Ham House. At the T-junction, turn left down Ham Street. After about 500 metres pass Sandy Lane.

15. At the end of Ham Street, turn right onto Lock Road and back onto NCN 4. Turn right onto Broughton Avenue. After the bus stop, turn sharp left down a shared path. Cross Hardwicke Road to the right onto another shared path. Cross Riverside Drive onto a further shared path to the left of a Thames Cycle Route signpost. This leads back to Teddington Lock's footbridge.

16. Turn left to follow the river on the right, staying on the upper path. About 0.6 miles from the weir, join Lower Ham Road.

17. Turn right, onto a path that runs between a park (Canbury Gardens) and the Thames. After 800 metres, leave the path and emerge onto Thameside. Turn left up Down Hall Road, using a green contra-flow cycle lane which bends around the corner into Skerne Road.

18. Pass under the railway bridge and turn left up onto the shared pavement to retrace the route back to Richmond station.

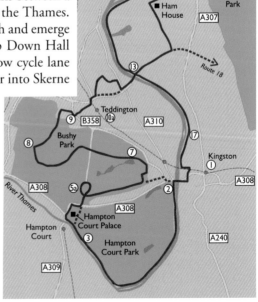

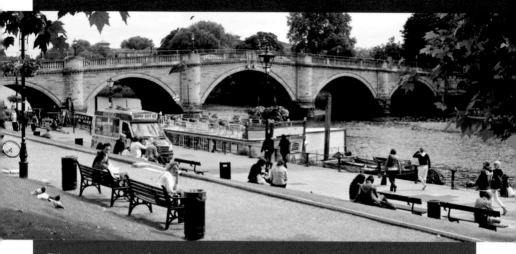

Distance: 5.65 miles starting and finishing from Ham Common. Add 3.25 miles if starting and finishing from Pembroke Lodge car park/0.95 miles if starting from Richmond station.

Map: Explorer 161 and TfL Local Cycling Guides 9 or 10.

Surface: Tarmac roads and gravel river paths that are mostly all weather. Tidal flooding around Petersham can be expected during exceptionally high tides and after prolonged periods of heavy rain. Route accessible via steps on Richmond Lock footbridge.

Surface and gradient: If starting or finishing at Richmond station, there is a short walk across the Quadrant (A307) onto quiet roads via an alleyway. Busy crossings worth noting are the Petersham Road (A307) at Ham Common and Petersham, and the Richmond Road (A305) near Richmond Bridge. Hammerton's Foot Ferry runs between Marble Hill Park and Ham House from March to October. (The service is not guaranteed, so ring to check on 0208 – 892 9620. There is a charge for crossing – £1.50 per person with a bike.)

Refreshments: At Pembroke Lodge, there is a snack bar that sells drinks, homemade ice cream and bacon/sausage rolls. There is also the New Inn pub at Ham Common and numerous possibilities along the Richmond riverfront.

This is a circular, mostly flat riverside ride north from the picturesque hamlet of Ham, following the Thames up to Richmond Lock. The route passes Richmond's riverside residential areas as well as the lively riverfront by Richmond Bridge.

BACKGROUND AND PLACES OF INTEREST

Ham House
Built in 1610 for Sir Thomas Vavasour, this palatial Thames-side residence was given to the National Trust in 1948. Its interior is rich in 17th- and 18th-century furniture, fine art and textiles, and its gardens – have changed little in 300 years. Ham House is said to be haunted by the Duchess of Lauderdale, who died there in 1698.

Hammerton's Ferry
This small pedestrian/cycle ferry, which crosses the Thames near Ham House, has been running for over 100 years and is very much a family affair. The current proud owners, Francis and Jenny Spencer, took over the service in 2003. (normally £1.50 including a bike).

Starting Points & Parking
1. Pembroke Lodge car park in Richmond Park (between Richmond and Ham Gate).
2. Ham Common
3. Richmond station - frequent services on South West Trains' Reading-Waterloo line. The North London Line runs from here to Stratford, and Richmond is also on a loop that includes Twickenham, Kingston, Wimbledon and Clapham Junction.
4. Free street parking around Ham Common, at the end of Ham Street, next to Ham House and further down by the river. The car park at Ham Close/off Ashburnham Road, is free, as is Pembroke Lodge car park.

Ham House.

Links to other routes

Route 01 – Kingston to Teddington Lock via Hampton Court Palace.
Route 18 – Richmond Park (via Nightingale Lane).
Route 03 – Richmond Lock to Kew Bridge loop.

ROUTE INSTRUCTIONS

Sandy Lane, towards the back of Ham House.

1. (A) From Pembroke Lodge car park in Richmond Park, turn left onto the sandy track (the 'Tamsin Trail'). Just before the crossroads, turn right and go downhill to Ham Gate. Join the road heading away from Richmond Park along Ham Gate Avenue. (B) From Richmond station, push your bike across the Quadrant (A307), using the pedestrian crossing, and take the alleyway to your right through to Parkshot. Turn left and continue straight to Friars Lane. Turn left on to Water Lane. Go to 7.

2. Take care crossing the busy Petersham Road (A307). Follow around the top of Ham Common. Just after St Michael's Convent, turn right onto the white gravel track and continue over Sandy Lane towards the back of Ham House, where there is a fantastic view of the building through the huge wrought iron gates. Turn left to continue around to the northern side of Ham House. The track gives way to a tarmac road before leading to a T-junction with Ham Street.

3. Turn right, heading down towards the river. This area may flood at certain times, so the route is sometimes very muddy or impassable. (Check the tidal status of the Thames.) Get onto the gravel river path and turn right.

4. After 350 yards, you will see a sign with a wooden platform and concrete steps leading down to the water. This is where you need to hail Hammerton's Ferry to cross over to the northern bank of the Thames. The ferry is based at the jetty on the other bank. If the tide is low, take care on the steps.

5. Turn right on leaving the jetty, onto the good tarmac surface of the pathway that runs along this side of the river. After a mile the track bends inland, joining the Richmond Road, with a pedestrian crossing that leads to Willoughby Road opposite. The next part of the route alternates between quiet sections of residential road and shared pathways. After passing under the railway bridge at Twickenham and Twickenham Bridge itself, you enter Ranelagh Drive. This stretch is also liable to flood at certain times.

Richmond Lock.

6. Dismount and carry your bike over Richmond Lock. Turn right and head south again, passing through Richmond's riverside frontage. The path here is an all-weather hard-packed surface. A short distance after the bridges, a row of bollards marks the path changing to the cobbled Water Lane. Here there is an option to turn left into Friar's Lane and join the signposted half-mile route on the Capital Ring to Richmond station. On busy weekend afternoons, it is advisable to dismount at this point and walk the 112 yards past the numerous pubs and bars until you emerge on the other side of Richmond Bridge.

7. The path enters a wooded area where it runs next to the A307 (Petersham Road). Looking to your left across the meadows, you will see the larger Star and Garter Home and the smaller Petersham Hotel. Keep heading along the straight towpath that reverts to a hard-packed gravel surface.

8. Take the first left away from the river up River Lane. Turn right onto Petersham Road (A307). After 120 yards, take the first right where you can see a large sign for Ham Polo Club. Consider walking this distance, remaining on the pavement from the end of River Lane to avoid crossing the busy narrow road.

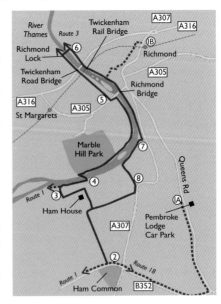

9. Keep to the right of the ornate gatehouse building and turn right to join the hard-packed path that runs down the middle of the avenue of trees. This runs all the way back past Ham Polo Club and the ornamental gate of Ham House. Now follow the white gravel track all the way back to Ham Common.

Distance: 6.3 miles.

Surface and Gradients: Generally a flat, river-plain ride on tarmac roads and gravel river paths that are mostly all weather. Tidal flooding can be expected during exceptionally high tides and after prolonged periods of heavy rain. Route accessible via steps on Richmond Lock footbridge.

Roads and road crossings: At Richmond station there is a short walk across the Quadrant (A307) onto quiet roads via an alleyway. In Isleworth there is a short section on the Richmond Road (A3004) and care is also needed at the A3004 junction between North and South Street. On the very busy Brentford High Street (A315), riders are advised to stick to the longer route away from the main road, and one section of Half Acre (A3002) can also be busy. At the complicated Kew Bridge junction of the A315 and A205, it may be advisable to walk over the pedestrian crossings.

Refreshments: Isleworth has the Apprentice riverside pub. There are tearooms (open weekends from mid-March to late October) in Syon House and several cafés on Brentford High Street. Kew Green has two excellent pubs. There is a café in Kew Gardens, but an entry fee is payable.

This is a riverside ride starting from Richmond Lock, heading north along the river before moving inland toward Syon House. There is a brief stint around the backstreets of Brentford to avoid the High Street before we rejoin the tranquillity of the Thames Path at Kew, where it heads south back to the lock.

BACKGROUND AND PLACES OF INTEREST

Kew Bridge Steam Museum
Housed in an impressive pumping station built in the 19th century, you can view the world's largest collection of steam-powered pump engines, ride on London's only steam railway and explore the fascinating history of water in London from Roman times to the present day.

Kew Gardens
The Royal Botanic Gardens is made up of 121 hectares. It is an internationally important botanical research and education institution. There are also numerous attractions to visit within the gardens, including the famous Palm House, Kew Palace, the Great Pagoda, the Princess of Wales Conservatory and the Water Lily House.

Syon Park
Syon House and its 200-acre park is the London home of the Duke and Duchess of Northumberland, whose family have lived there for over 400 years. Its plain exterior hides a superlative Robert Adam interior built in 1762, on the site of a medieval abbey, surrounded by 55 acres of gardens begun by Capability Brown.

Starting Points & Parking
1. Richmond station – frequent services on South West Trains' Reading-Waterloo line. The North London Line runs from here to Stratford, and Richmond is also on a loop that includes Twickenham, Kingston, Wimbledon and Clapham Junction.
2. Kew Bridge station – services on South West Trains' Hounslow Loop line that includes Waterloo, Weybridge Putney and Barnes.
3. Richmond station. On-street parking is permit controlled.
4. Friars Lane car park. Limited to 4 hours (£7.50).
5. Kew Bridge station. There is a multi-storey car park at Paradise Road (£15 per day/£3 Sunday).
6. Kew Gardens car park. £4.50 per day.

Links to other routes
Route 02 – Ham Common to Richmond Lock loop.
Route 12 – the Grand Union Canal: Paddington branch to Brentford Lock.
Route 18 – Richmond Park.

ROUTE INSTRUCTIONS:

1. From Richmond station wheel your bike across the Quadrant (A307) using the pedestrian crossing and take the alleyway to your right through to Parkshot. Continue straight ahead past Richmond Green.

2. Carry straight on to Friars Lane, which twists and turns all the way to the riverside path.

3. Turn right onto the riverside path, passing under the rail and road bridges to Richmond Lock footbridge. Dismount and cross the lock. Turn right and follow the path where the road bends away from the river. The track is tarmac but it's rough and rutted, and can flood in places.

4. The path joins Railshead Road and heads away from the river up to Richmond Road. Turn right. The bus stop on the left and the bend in the road can make emerging dangerous, so take care. Enter a short cycle lane before taking the first left on the bend and then turning right along the quieter service road until rejoining Richmond Road.

5. Turn left at the mini-roundabout where the cycle lane ends. Take the first right onto North Street. (It may be safer to dismount and cross where there is a break in the traffic.) Continue up North Street on the bend, but do not follow the road right where it becomes Swan Street.

6. Turn first right into Manor House Way, leading to the Georgian terraced houses of Church Street and finally back to the river/the Apprentice pub.

7. Just after the road bends away from the river, turn right into Syon Park. Follow the cycle path across the car park and up a shared path that opens out into a road. There is a further cycle path that leads to the busy London Road (A315) and a Toucan crossing.

View of Church Street, Isleworth, from the south bank. Eileen Sheridan, champion English cyclist of the 1940s and 50s, lived in Church Street. Her 1954 London to Edinburgh record of 20h 11m 35s has yet to be beaten.

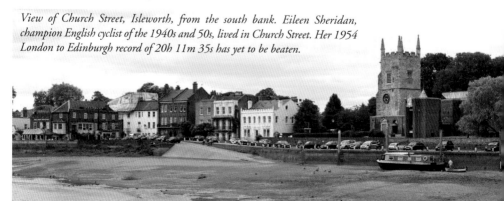

8. Turn right and proceed along the cycle lane. This is the worst part of the route but it does not last long. More experienced cyclists may choose to push on towards Kew Bridge on the A315 and skip to point 12. The less experienced may be better suited to taking the back roads.

9. Take the first left after crossing the Grand Union Canal into Tallow Road. Dismount and cross the pavement for the first right into Market Place, which becomes Lions Way. Turn right and then left into the supermarket car park between the police station and the Beehive pub. Dismount for the very short alleyway that leads to a left turn onto St Paul's Road.

10. At the T-junction, turn right in front of the church and follow the road around the park. Turn left into Brook Road South, then first right onto Braemer Road. Turn right then left across Ealing Road onto Netley Road, which becomes Clayponds Lane.

11. Turn right onto Green Dragon Lane. This meets with the A315 at the point where the Kew Bridge Steam Museum is on the corner. The more experienced rider may choose the red cycle lane in the middle of the complicated Kew Bridge junction to turn right. The less cavalier should cross via the numerous pedestrian crossings. For Kew Bridge station, turn and keep left for 150 metres. If starting the route here, exit the station, turn right and push your bike along the footpath. Use the pedestrian crossing to reach the bridge.

12. Over the bridge, take the first left after the pedestrian crossing onto Kew Green. Take the hairpin bend onto Waterloo Place and the river path beneath Kew Bridge Road, which can be very bumpy in places.

13. If you choose to break up the ride and have a picnic in Kew Gardens, there is an entrance at the end of the car park. Now you can enjoy 1.8 miles of wild riverside path back to Richmond Lock.

Distance: 3.7 miles.

Map: Ordnance Survey Explorer map 161 and TfL Local Cycling Guide 6.

Surface and Gradients: Flat tarmac roads and gravel river paths that are mostly all weather. Tidal flooding can be expected during exceptionally high tides and after prolonged periods of heavy rain. Route accessible via steps on both sides of the Barnes Railway Bridge footpath.

Roads and road crossings: The road around Strand on the Green can be busy at the time of the school run. Kew Bridge is particularly bad for cyclists, with no cycle lane or shared path. The short section of road on The Terrace, before Barnes Bridge station, is both narrow and busy. Consider walking this 200-metre section and enjoying the view of the Thames.***

Refreshments: The area around Strand on the Green has three good pubs – The Bull's Head, The City Barge and The Bell and Crown – with riverside views, as has The Ship on Thames Bank/Ship Lane. The White Hart is perfectly placed for a well deserved refreshment stop at the end of the route. Barnes High Street close to Barnes Bridge station has many refreshment possibilities.

Chiswick Bridge, as viewed from the south bank.

This route is a short circular ride along the north and south sides of the Thames. The north side is mainly on quiet residential roads and the south side is mainly on the riverbank. Although this section does not boast major tourist attractions like the other Thames routes, it does brim with the charm of west London's Thames-side character.

BACKGROUND AND PLACES OF INTEREST

Barnes Railway Bridge

One of only three bridges in London that combine rail and pedestrian use, and it actually comprises two bridges built side by side. The original bridge was built in 1849, the replacement bridge in 1895, and a major refurbishment was completed in 2010, when 16,000 square metres of wrought iron trusses and arches on the Grade II listed bridge were cleaned and repainted.

Chiswick Bridge

One of three bridges built in the early 1930s to relieve west London's traffic congestion, it feeds the Great Chertsey Road from Chiswick on the north bank to Mortlake on the south bank. Designed by Sir Herbert Baker, the 700-foot-long bridge comprises three flat ferro-concrete arches faced with Portland stone.

Kew Bridge

The first bridge, built by Robert Tunstall, was opened in 1759 when over 3000 people crossed in one day. The second was designed by James Paine, also responsible for Richmond Bridge, and built entirely of stone whereas the first contained 7 timber arches. It was opened in 1789. When it became obvious that it couldn't cope with the volume of traffic, the third and present bridge was designed by John Wolfe-Barry and opened in 1903.

Starting Points & Transport:

1. Barnes Bridge station. Rail services on South West Trains' Hounslow Loop line that includes Waterloo, Weybridge Putney and Kew Bridge. There is parking in some residential roads in Barnes and Sundays are free.

2. Dukes Meadow (near Chiswick Bridge). There is some free parking in Dan Mason Drive, just east of the bridge.

Links to other routes
Route 05 – Putney Bridge to Barnes Bridge loop.
Route 03 – Richmond Lock to Richmond via Kew Bridge.

ROUTE INSTRUCTIONS:

1. Exit Barnes Bridge station from platform one and cross over the Thames. At the bottom of the steps on the north bank, turn left and cycle up the path that runs away from the river parallel. Join Riverside Drive and follow it straight ahead under the railway lines and back along the edge of Dukes Meadow. The road turns away from the Thames at the Tideway Scullers' boathouse.

2. At the traffic lights, cross the Great Chertsey Road (A316) onto the quieter Hartington Road, continuing straight ahead for 1 kilometre.

3. At the mini-roundabout, turn left into Grove Park Road. The road turns inland and follows into Thames Road. The river reappears on the left after the Bell and Crown pub, where the road becomes Strand on the Green and leads up to Kew Bridge.

4. Turn sharp left at the traffic lights onto the footpath over Kew Bridge, or walk up the steps from Strand on the Green. Walk across the bridge or risk the traffic. Turn left onto Kew Green and take the very sharp left onto Waterloo Place. Follow it around to the Thames. This is the start of an uninterrupted 0.8-mile path passing Oliver's Island, Kew Railway Bridge and the National Archives on the way to Chiswick Bridge, 1.25 miles away.

5. Pass under the bridge and join Thames Bank. On the corner opposite the Ship pub, take the path that runs between the brewery and the river. It will be very muddy in winter and difficult to ride at very high tides, in which case carry on along Ship Lane and turn left to follow the frequently busy A3003 eastwards.

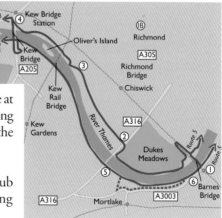

6. Emerge from behind the White Hart pub to join the road again. Turn left along The Terrace to Barnes Bridge station.

ROUTE 5
Putney Bridge to Barnes Bridge loop

Distance: 8 miles.

Map: Ordnance Survey Explorer 161 and TfL Local Cycling Guide 6.

Surface and Gradients: Generally a mixture of flat shared paths and minor roads, but the route also conjoins three times with busier roads. Tidal flooding is possible along sections of the riverside path during exceptionally high tides and after prolonged periods of heavy rain. Chiswick Mall (after Hammersmith Bridge) is particularly susceptible. Barnes Bridge has steps.

Roads and road crossings: The route between Putney station and Putney Bridge (A219) is 560 metres long and constantly very busy.*** The buses along this narrow stretch of road are intimidating for most cyclists, and a 100-metre section of the busy Hammersmith Bridge Road (A306) that may also require walking. There is also a busy 560-metre section from Barnes Bridge to the riverside path off Lonsdale Road (B350).

Refreshments: Pryor's Bank Café is just inside Bishops Park and there is also a café in the nearby Fulham Palace. There are numerous good pubs along the river after Hammersmith Bridge. The cafés of Barnes High Street are a short diversion from the mini-roundabout after Barnes Bridge.

This route follows most of the boat race course. It starts at minor roads and shared Thames paths before a long stretch of wooded or grassy path. After a brief encounter with traffic after Barnes Bridge, the ride finishes with a wonderful 2.65-mile off-road run down to the Embankment at Putney Bridge. It is advisable to check online that there is not a Head of the River rowing race being held.

BACKGROUND AND PLACES OF INTEREST

Fulham Palace

The oldest and most important building in Hammersmith and Fulham. Formerly the country home of the Bishops of London, it can be traced back to about 700AD. It sits in a historic garden, a fascinating mixture of architectural styles from Tudor to Victorian: a medieval great hall with a 16th-century courtyard to the west, an 18th-century courtyard to the east and a 19th-century chapel to the south. There is also a small museum and a gallery of contemporary art. Admission is free.

The Griffin Brewery, Chiswick

This Fuller's brewery has been brewing beer on the site since the time of Oliver Cromwell, over 350 years ago. A large part of the historic early Victorian brewhouse, part of John Fuller's original investment, can be viewed preserved within the current brewhouse. Within the records store, Fuller's have original brewing logbooks dating from the latter part of the 19th century. The Griffin Brewery is open to the public for official tours.

Starting Points & Transport:

1. Putney station – via South West Trains' Waterloo-Windsor line and the Hounslow loop line. Parking is possible on many roads on the estate just off Putney Heath, and is free across Putney on Sundays.
2. Barnes Bridge station via South West Trains' Hounslow loop line. There is free parking along the Promenade on the Middlesex bank of the Thames, near Barnes Bridge, and in some residential roads around Barnes.

As this is a circular route it can be joined at any point.

Links to other routes

Route 04 – Barnes Bridge to Kew Bridge loop.
Route 06 – Battersea to Putney Bridge via Chelsea Harbour.

ROUTE INSTRUCTIONS:

1. Exit Putney station. Turn right to cross at the traffic lights before cycling along Putney High Street (A219). Continue across Putney Bridge. Turn left into Bishops Park just before All Saints Church.

2. Cycling is not permitted on the path next to the river here, so follow along the avenue of trees. The route twists and turns before it runs parallel to Stevenage Road, where the park ends.

3. Just after passing Fulham FC's ground, take the first left down the pathway to walk along the signposted Thames River Path, before rejoining the ride via Crabtree Lane on Rainville Road. If staying on your bike, turn right into Meadow Bank Close and first left into Holyport Road.

4. Turn right into Crabtree Lane. On the bend take the cycle path to Petley Road. At the end turn left onto Wingrave Road and then right onto Rainville Road.

5. At the end of the road, where it turns right into Colwith Road, take the left-hand path that leads to the river path. Join Chancellor's Road then take the first left into Crisp Road, passing the famous Riverside Studios arts centre. At the T-junction turn right into Queen Caroline Street and then first left into Worlidge Street.

6. Turn left onto Hammersmith Bridge Road. The bus lane offers some protection from the traffic, but you may feel safer using the pedestrian crossing and pushing your bike the short distance to turn right into Rutland Grove. Cycle straight ahead into Furnival Gardens. Follow the path through the middle of the park, to the alleyway which passes the Drove pub, and onto Upper Mall.

7. As Upper Mall bends right and becomes Oil Mill Lane, carry on along the Thames Path until entering a little park and then veer to the right following the path onto Chiswick Mall (with its small islet in the Thames called Chiswick Eyot). This part of the route is liable to be flooded at times. Shortly after the Griffin Brewery, leave Chiswick Mall where it turns away from the Thames and becomes Church Street.

Bishops Park.

8. Proceed down the shared pathway to Pumping Station Road and continue until the roundabout, taking the second left into Thames Crescent. The path to the left of the big wrought iron gates leads back to the river path. The path is narrow and often busy here, and so walking may be appropriate.

9. Turn left onto The Promenade, passing the Civil Service Sports Grounds on your right. As the road passes behind a boathouse, turn left onto the footpath leading to the steps to Barnes Bridge. On the other side, use the pedestrian crossing to turn right along The Terrace (A3003).

10. Go straight over the mini-roundabout onto Lonsdale Road. Past the car park, turn left to rejoin the river path. It is sandy and hard packed if a little rutted in places, and is still easy to ride in the winter. Enjoy the glorious leafy path for 1.35 miles to Hammersmith Bridge. Carry on for a further 1.3 miles before returning to the road again at the Embankment, following all the way to Putney Pier and onto Lower Richmond Road (B306).

11. Turn left and then right at the traffic lights along the very busy Putney High Street. The road splits at the next set of lights; get onto the incredibly narrow cycle lane that runs down the middle. Continue straight up to Putney station.

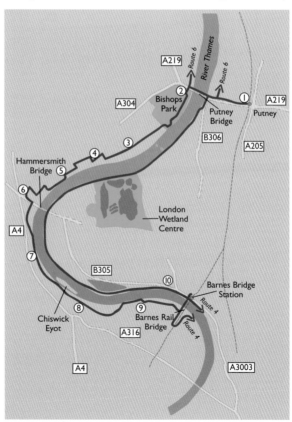

ROUTE 6
Battersea to Putney Bridge via Chelsea Harbour

Distance: 10.75 miles, if starting and finishing at Clapham Junction.

Map: Ordnance Survey Explorer map 161 and TfL Local Cycling Guide 7.

Surface and Gradients: Flat sealed roads and paths.

Roads and road crossings: If starting from Battersea Park station, Queenstown Road (A3216) is frequently busy, so it is recommended to walk the 300 metres to the park. If starting from Clapham Junction, take care crossing Prince of Wales Drive. Chelsea Bridge Road is often busy, but cautious riders can follow the Thames west on the shared path along the riverside pavement. Crossing Putney Bridge can be intimidating; alternatively cross the Thames on the footpath along the Fulham railway bridge, though there are steps to negotiate. The industrial section after crossing the Wandle River will be quiet on weekends and Bank Holidays.

Refreshments: The Eight Bells (near Putney Bridge station) and the Boathouse (on Brew House Lane) are worth a mention. Battersea Park has an excellent café, La Gondola Al Parco, and there are also ice-cream kiosks Carriage Drive North. The area around Putney Bridge station has cafes and a very good baguette shop. Pryor's Bank Café is just inside Bishops Park, next to Putney Bridge (northside).

The main attraction of this circular route is the 200-acre Battersea Park. With its wide closed roads, the park is ideal for cycling with young children, especially if a visit to the children's zoo and boating lake are factored in. Older visitors can do a circuit of the park, stopping at the Peace Pagoda before a walk around the lake to look at the sculptures or a visit to the Pump House Gallery.

BACKGROUND AND PLACES OF INTEREST

Battersea Park

Battersea Fields became a park over a 12-year period, finished in 1858 after using a reputed million cubic feet of soil (from the construction of Victoria Docks) to raise the land and protect it from the tides of the Thames. The huge lake, with its three islands, was added during the 1860s; the Cascades were created shortly after, to give the impression of a geological fault revealing sandstone rocks.

Chelsea Bridge

The second to be built on the site of an ancient ford. The current bridge was opened in 1937. It was the first self-anchored suspension bridge in Britain.

Starting Points & Transport:

1. Clapham Junction station. Check online for the numerous services available.
2. Battersea Park – station accessible via Southern Trains services from Victoria. Pay and display car parks in Battersea Park at £1.20 per hour/£4 all day Sundays on Carriage Drive South, North and West.

Links to other routes

Route 05 – Putney Bridge to Barnes Bridge loop.
Route 15 – Mitcham Junction to Wandsworth (The Wandle Trail: Part Two).

ROUTE INSTRUCTIONS:

1. A) Exit Clapham Junction station via Grant Road (near Platform 1) and turn right. At the T-junction with Falcon Road, turn left onto the pavement cycle lane. Take the toucan crossing and then take the first right into Este Road. Turn left onto a shared path into Wayford Street (sign for London Cycle Network Route 37). Turn right onto Cabul Road. Continue

The Peace Pagoda, Battersea Park.

under the rail bridge and take the shared path to the left. Pass under two railway bridges and emerge onto Latchmere Road. Use the toucan crossing and turn right into Burns Road. At the T-junction, turn right onto Reform Street. Turn left at the T-junction onto Sheepcote Lane, which bends left into Culvert Road, and take the first right into Rowditch Lane. At the end of the road take the right-hand path, parallel with the railway embankment. After 280 metres turn left to join Rawson Street, leading to the toucan crossing over the very busy Battersea Park Road (A3205). Continue up Macduff Road, cross over Prince of Wales Drive and enter Battersea Park.

1. B) Exit Battersea Park station at street level onto Battersea Park Road. Turn right to walk (recommended) the 300 metres to Rosary Gate. Turn right then right again onto Queenstown Road and continue up to Queens Circus roundabout. Rosary Gate is on the far left.

2. From Rosary Gate car park, continue cycling around the park in an anti-clockwise direction. Once a circuit has been completed, go back to the car park and walk around the lake clockwise to rejoin the road near the La Gondola Al Parco café. Turn left and exit the park via Chelsea Gate. Turn left to take the shared path over the bridge to the north bank of the Thames and the very busy Chelsea Embankment (A3213).

3. Dismount and use the pedestrian crossing to Chelsea Bridge Road (A3216), heading north of the river. Cautious riders may choose instead to cycle along the shared path (NCN 4) on the Thames north bank, towards Chelsea Harbour. (In which case skip to 5.) Once past the bus stop there is a narrow cycle lane. Pass the Royal Hospital Chelsea and turn left at the traffic lights onto Royal Hospital Road (B302). Pass the entrances for the National Army Museum and the Chelsea Physic Garden on the left. Royal Hospital Road bends around to meet Chelsea Embankment at traffic lights.

4. Use the toucan crossing to get to the shared path along the Thames and turn right.

5. Pass the Albert Bridge onto Cheyne Walk. After Battersea Bridge the path narrows considerably as it passes the houseboats

Single Form by Barbara Hepworth, in Battersea Park.

on Cheyne Pier. The shared path ends leads straight onto Lots Road. Passing the power station, turn left at the mini-roundabout onto Chelsea Harbour Drive.

Royal Hospital Chelsea.

6. Take the road between the yellow barriers towards the Wyndham Grand luxury apartment block. At the next automatic road barrier, dismount to walk down the path to the harbour (cycling is not permitted). After a circuit of the harbour on foot, return to Harbour Avenue but turn left to follow the road around. Turn right at the mini-roundabout to go under the railway bridge, along The Boulevard and onto Townmead Road. The traffic can be heavy, so be alert.

7. Turn right into Bagley Lane. If the traffic is heavy use the pedestrian island to cross. Turn left into Elswick Street. At the T-junction, turn left onto Stephendale Road (to the right of the church) and follow to the crossing with Wandsworth Bridge Road (A217). Dismount to use the zebra crossing to cross this busy arterial road. Cycle down Hugon Road to the end. Turn right and immediate left into Sulivan Road. At the end turn right onto Broomhouse Lane. At the top of the park, follow the road to the left onto Hurlingham Road. Take the first left into Napier Road and turn right onto Ranelagh Gardens.

8. Pass under the railway bridge. Putney Bridge station is on the right. The road bends right into Fulham High Street; take the first left onto Gonville Street. (To avoid the busy Putney Bridge area dismount and walk down the alley just after passing under the railway bridge. Climb the steps and cross the Fulham Railway Bridge. Pick up the main route again on Deodar Road, Step 9.)

9. Turn left to cross Putney Bridge (A219). On the south side of the bridge, take the first left into Putney Bridge Road (B3209). Either take the next left into Brewhouse Street to visit the Boathouse pub or enjoy the riverside views north of the Thames. Walk down the alleyway that runs next to the pub, onto Deodar Road, or alternatively take the second left.

10. Where Deodar Road bends right, dismount and walk through Blade Mews to enter Wandsworth Park. Cycle again left up to the riverside and along the wide avenue of trees.

11. Leave the park joining the red cycle lane. Where it ends the rider has two choices. To dismount and carry on, walking the 500 metres along the Thames riverside to Bell Lane Creek. Otherwise turn right, away from the river, onto Point Pleasant, and turn left onto Osiers Road and first right into the Enterprise Way industrial estate. Pass between the trees at the end to cross Bell Lane Creek. This is the confluence of the Wandle River and the end of Route 15 (Mitcham Junction to Putney).

12. Carry on straight ahead into Smugglers Way. After 300 metres, just before the big junction , turn left into Marl Road. Turn right at the mini-roundabout and then immediate left onto the cycle path leading to the Wandsworth Bridge roundabout.

13. Go down the ramp under the hanging billboard in the centre of the roundabout. Take the left-hand fork and climb up the ramp back to street level. Head south under the big railway bridge adjacent to Trinity Road (A214). Turn left from the dual carriageway, uphill to Nantes Close. This part of the route is on London Network 37.

14. After 200 metres, turn left onto the cycle lane to go back under the railway lines and take the immediate right onto Wynter Street. Take the first right onto Maysoule Road. At the end of the road, join the green cycle lane to the right and take the toucan crossing over Plough Road. Continue straight along Thomas Baines Road. Leave the road to pass between the tower blocks and turn right up Winstanley Road. Turn left onto Grant Road to end the route at Clapham Junction station. Go to (1) if you started from Battersea Park.

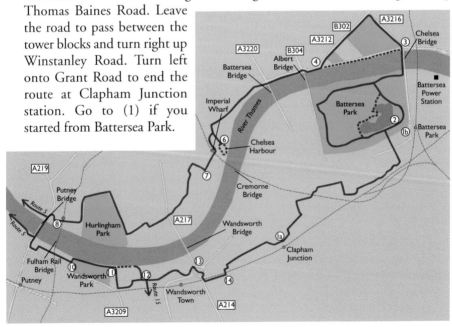

Distance: 2.3 miles.

Map: Ordnance Survey Explorer map 173 and TfL Local Cycling Guides 1 or 7.

Surface and Gradients: Flat ride on sealed roads. There are many sections on cobbled roads that can be slippery in the wet.

Roads and road crossings: There are a few busy junctions but with provision for cyclists and pedestrians to cross safely. The short section on Southwark Street after Blackfriars Road is worth walking. Tooley Street has a cycle lane but can be very busy at times.

Refreshments: The whole riverside area, especially around the Southbank and London Bridge, has many restaurants and cafés. There are numerous pubs along the route, some of which are on the riverside.

This is a linear route that travels from Waterloo eastwards to Tower Bridge. It is not yet possible to ride on the riverfront along this section, but there are many glimpses of the river down alleyways and paths. There are too many tourist landmarks to list in the route guide, so just keep looking around.

BACKGROUND AND PLACES OF INTEREST

Tower Bridge

One of the most iconic tourist attractions in London, Tower Bridge was completed in 1894. In order to provide 135 feet of shipping headroom it was designed with twin lifting sections or 'bascules', although these days it is fairly unusual to see the bridge open. It was built in Victorian Gothic style to blend in with the nearby Tower of London.

Tate Modern

The building that now houses the museum of international modern and contemporary art (moved in 2000 from what is now Tate Britain) was originally Bankside Power Station. It is a stark and imposing brick building with a 325-foot chimney, now one of the most popular art galleries in the world.

The Golden Hinde

The Golden Hinde

Visitors can sample a taste of Tudor life onboard London's full-sized replica of the Tudor warship in which Sir Francis Drake circumnavigated the globe, in 1577–80. It was built by traditional methods in Devon and, like the original, has sailed more than 140,000 miles since its launch in 1973. It has been berthed in St Mary Overie Dock in Bankside since 1996. The Golden Hinde is open daily between 10.00am and 5.30pm.

Starting Points & Transport:

1. Waterloo station – accessible via South West Trains services south and west of London. There are multi-storey car parks around the Southbank for £14 per day. Parking in the streets around the station is generally free and can be plentiful on Sundays and Bank Holidays.
2. London Bridge Station – Southern, South Eastern and First Capital Connect services south and east of London.

Links to other routes
Route 08 – Tower Bridge to Greenwich.
Route 09 – Tower Bridge to Limehouse Basin loop.
Route 20 – Hyde Park and The Mall

ROUTE INSTRUCTIONS:

1. Leave Waterloo Station via the exit opposite Platforms 12/13. On the opposite side of the road is a cycle lane marked by a high granite curb. Follow the cycle lane downhill over York Road (A3200) and under the train bridge on the shared pathway. Dismount when you get to the road and turn left, walking along Concert Hall Approach for 65 metres before turning right onto Belverdere Road.

2. Continue straight into Upper Ground (after Waterloo Bridge) all the way to the T-junction with Blackfriars Road (A201). Use the signposted NCN 4 crossing, where the cycle path runs unusually down the centre of the dual carriageway. At the end, use the pedestrian crossing to turn left and walk 150 metres up Southwark Street, under the rail bridge. Turn left into Hopton Street.

3. The road bends to the right to face the imposing Tate Modern gallery. Follow Holland Street up to turn left onto Summer Street. On the next bend turn left onto Park Street. There is a footpath on the next left that leads around to the front of Tate Modern and the Millennium Footbridge. The route now enters a contra-flow cycle lane.

4. Turn left into New Globe Walk for a short diversion to the Globe theatre and riverside views.

5. Continue on Park Street, passing under Southwark Bridge Road (A300) and the landmarked original site of the Globe. At the T-junction, turn left into Bank End and then right into Clink Street. Pass under the Cannon Street rail bridge. The road is very narrow here and often busy with tourists, so it may be necessary to dismount.

6. Continue to the end of the road. Walk around to the right of Golden Hind, then cycle again on Cathedral Street. Turn sharp left up Montague Place. Pass under the King William Street bridge

On Upper Ground, passing Oxo Tower Wharf.

Tower Bridge, seen from Pottersfield Park.

(A3) that runs over London Bridge, where the road runs into Tooley Street. At the T-junction opposite London Bridge station turn left. Take either Battle Bridge Lane or Hayes Lane down the side of Hayes Galleria to get to the Thames footpath and a fine view of HMS Belfast. If Tooley Street is too intimidating, follow the Thames path on foot to Tower Bridge.

7. Continue straight ahead for another 350 metres. Turn off the road and walk into Pottersfield Park through the girder-like arch. There are spectacular views of Tower Bridge, the Tower of London and City Hall. Route 08 – Tower Bridge to Greenwich – also passes here. To join with Route 09 – Tower Bridge to Limehouse Basin loop – take the steps up to the road across the bridge or cycle on Tooley Street. Take the first left onto Queen Elizabeth Street and the compulsory left turn to cross Tower Bridge.

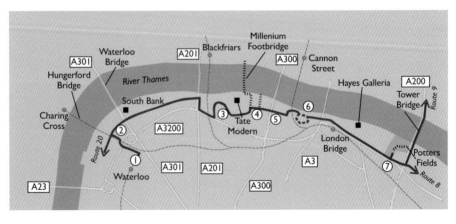

ROUTE 8
Tower Bridge to Greenwich

Distance: 6.7 miles to Greenwich station.

Map: Ordnance Survey Explorer map 173 and TfL Local Cycling Guide 7.

Surfaces and Gradients: This is a flat ride on sealed roads. There are frequent sections of cobbles that can be slippery in the wet.

Roads and road crossings: Tooley Street can be busy but there is a cycle lane. Grove Street has speed humps. The 200-metre stretch of Creek Road (A200) approaching Greenwich is on NCN Route 4, but the only provision is a shared bus, taxi and bike lane that runs out just before the route turns off.

Refreshments: The area around London Bridge station offers much choice, as does Greenwich. There are numerous good pubs and a few cafés as well as frequent corner-shops. This area of London is very much the dormitory for the masses who work across the water on the Isle of Dogs or up in the West End. The route starts near the old warehouses and wharfs converted into desirable apartment blocks, following NCN Route 04 until Rotherhithe – one of London's hidden gems, lovingly preserved around the docks. Rich in history and architecture, the Rotherhithe peninsula boasts some of the best views of London's iconic skylines. The tone changes at the Surrey Docks, where the architecture is predominantly the result of recent redevelopment.

BACKGROUND AND PLACES OF INTEREST

Greenland Dock

Originally known as Howland Great Wet Dock and once part of the Surrey Commercial Docks, it dates back to the late 1600s. During the 18th century the Greenland whale-fishery vessels docked at Rotherhithe, giving the dock its current name.

Greenland Dock.

Brunel Museum

On the site of the Thames Tunnel, the first to be built with a tunnelling shield under a navigable river, as designed by Sir Marc Brunel and assisted by his son Isambard. When it opened in 1843, people came from far and wide to see it.

Surrey Docks Farm

A working city farm in the heart of London, occupying a 2.2-acre site. Milking goats, sheep, cattle, pigs, ducks, geese, chickens, turkeys, bees and donkeys are all reared at the farm, with particular attention to animal welfare.

Starting Points & Transport:

1. Potters Fields next to Tower Bridge
2. London Bridge station – accessible via Southern, South Eastern and First Capital Connect services south and east of London.
3. There is a multi-storey car park at Butlers Wharf, 46-50 Gainsford Street, SE1, at £12 per day.
4. Greenwich station – South Eastern train services on the London Cannon Street to Slade Green Line. Also services from London Bridge, Charing Cross and Waterloo East stations.

Links to other routes

Route 07 – Waterloo to Tower Bridge.
Route 09 – Tower Bridge to Limehouse Basin Loop.
Route 13 – The Isle of Dogs.
Route 16 – The Waterlink Way.

ROUTE INSTRUCTIONS

1. Exit London Bridge station. Use the pedestrian crossing to turn right onto Tooley Street. Follow the cycle lane. Shortly past Potters Fields, take the left turn off the cycle path onto Queen Elizabeth Street and across Tower Bridge Road. Pass through The Circle – a circular building clad with deep blue glazed tiles – and by a huge bronze horse statue in the centre of the road. At the T-junction, turn right to continue along Shad Thames.

2. At the traffic lights, turn left onto Jamaica Road (A200). Turn left at the second of two junctions into Dockhead. Go past the small parade of shops as the road bends to the right, turning left into Parker's Row. At the T-junction opposite the fire station, turn right onto Wolseley Street.

3. Turn left onto George Row, right onto Chambers Street and take the third left into Loftie Street. At the end, turn right onto Bermondsey Wall East. There are plenty of places to walk up to the river's edge for views across the Thames.

4. Continue, leave the road and join a sealed path across open ground. The path goes around some terraced housing on the water's edge, then out into Elephant Lane. Turn left to follow the river. As Elephant Lane bends inland to the right, take the alleyway straight ahead.

5. Emerge onto Rotherhithe Street, passing the Mayflower Pub on the left and Brunel Museum on the right. Leave NCN Route 04 here and stay on Rotherhithe Street. Pass through the red bascule bridge, the entrance to Surrey Basin and what used to be the Surrey Docks complex.

6. Rotherhithe Street continues with views of Docklands and Canary Wharf. The next bridge passes over the entrance to Lavender Pond Nature Park. After the Blacksmith's Arms pub and the Hilton hotel, turn left up the steep ramp into Durand's Wharf Park, where there are views of the Docklands skyline. Return to the road, turning left.

7. Stay on Rotherhithe Street, bending around Surrey Docks Farm. Turn left at the junction, continuing along the same road. Turn left into Odessa Street, following it to the end (don't turn right into Gulliver Street) to join the shared path and turn left towards the Thames, where the route rejoins NCN Route 4.

The huge statue in the centre of The Circle on Queen Elizabeth Street.

8. Pass around Helsinki Square and turn left to cross the bridge over the entrance to Greenland Dock. Turn left onto Rope Street, follow past the ferry terminal and continue straight ahead, leaving the road to walk over South Dock lock.

9. Turn left back to the river's edge, keeping it on your left for the next 650 metres. Pass the boatyard and continue along Deptford Wharf. After passing Aragon Tower, rejoin the road to follow Deptford Strand around the corner of the flats.

10. Follow the path straight across the park. Dismount and go down the steps; there is a special flat ramp along the left side to wheel your bike. Cross the next park around the left-hand side to join Grove Street, turning left.

11. Turn left off the road into Sayes Court Gardens. Stay to the right of the park, pass around the children's playground and out into Sayes Court Street. Take the first left into Decca Street, continue down to the T-junction with Prince Street and turn left again, re-entering an area of industrial wharfs and warehouses.

12. Continue to the T-junction with Watergate Street and turn left, where it runs into cobbled Borthwick Street on the next bend. Just after the electricity substation (with redbrick star pattern), leave the road to join a path around the yacht club.

13. The path rejoins the waterfront and bends inland up Deptford Creek (see Route 16), finally joining Creek Road (A200) at a toucan crossing. Turn left using the shared bike, bus and taxi lane, then turn first left into Norway Street. Turn right onto Thames Street and second left into Horseferry Place. At the end of the road, pass through the bollards to join the riverside path leading to the Cutty Sark and Greenwich Foot Tunnel, where this route joins Route 26.

14. Retrace the route down Norway Street but cross over Creek Road and take the immediate left onto Haddo Street. Pass between barriers to follow this road and turn left into Randall Place. Turn right onto Straightmouth. Continue to the end and take the path across to Tarves Way. Go up the ramp to Platform One of Greenwich station.

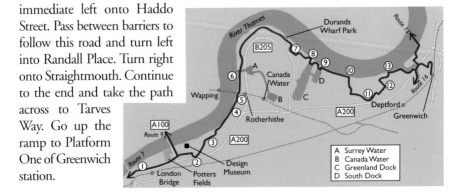

ROUTE 9
Tower Bridge to Limehouse Basin loop

Distance: 2.4 miles. Add 1.5 miles if returning to Tower Bridge via Cable Street. Add 0.85 miles if starting from London Bridge station. Add half a mile if starting from Fenchurch Street station.

Map: Ordnance Survey Explorer map 173 and TfL Local Cycling Guide 7.

Surface and Gradients: This is a flat all-weather route, frequently along the water's edge. The ride is on tarmac roads, frequently cobbled near the start. There are also paved or tarmac paths.

Roads and road crossings: From Fenchurch Street station Minories and Goodman's Yard can be very busy so may be better walked. Care is needed at the busy section on Bucher Row, between the pedestrian crossing on the Limehouse Link road and Cable Street. The route from Royal Mint Street to St Katherine's Way can also be very busy, although these junctions have traffic lights and left turns, which are safer. It is also short enough to walk at 200 metres.***

Refreshments: St Katherine's Dock has restaurants, cafés and pubs. The Grapes Pub (76) and Booty's Riverside Bar (92a) in Narrow Street are well placed towards the end of the route.

This circular route is surprisingly quiet apart from the short section near Tower Bridge, joining together the hubs of the old dock and canal systems. While thousands of tourists flock to the Tower of London and Tower Bridge, few seem to venture along the canal or river paths just a stone's throw away.

BACKGROUND AND PLACES OF INTEREST

St Katherine's Dock

Named after the 12th-century priory hospital (St Katharine's by the Tower) that was demolished to make way for it in 1827. The great engineer Thomas Telford designed the docks using two basins to give as much quayside as possible, but St Katherine's Dock always struggled due to not accommodating large ships. Severely damaged by bombing during the Second World War, it never really recovered, finally closing in 1968. In the 1970s many of the original quayside warehouses were demolished and the old dock was developed as a marina.

Shadwell Basin

Shadwell Dock is a prominent reminder of the London docks' historic past. The Shadwell Basin used to connect the Eastern Dock in Wapping to the Thames. Its two massive red bascule bridges were a prominent feature of the basin, rising to allow ships to enter the dock. The dock closed in 1969 and fell into disrepair, before redevelopment of the Shadwell Basin took place in 1987.

Looking east across the Shadwell Basin, the most historically significant body of water surviving from the London Docks.

Limehouse Basin

This is the gateway to the River Lea Navigation, described in detail in Route 17.

Starting Points & Transport:

1. London Bridge station – accessible via Southern, South Eastern and First Capital Connect services south and east of London.
2. Parking at BCP, Butlers Wharf, 46-50 Gainsford Street, SE1 (£12 per day). Street parking is free and plentiful at weekends.
3. Fenchurch Street station – accessible via c2c services to East London and South Essex.
4. Parking at St Katherine's Way, Burr Close, E1 (£16 per day) and the NCP at Thomas More Square, 1 Nesham Street, E1 (£13 per weekday/£7.80 at weekends).

Looking east along the canal, which is all that remains of the vast West Dock.

Links to other routes:

Route 07 – Waterloo to Tower Bridge.
Route 08 – Tower Bridge to Greenwich.
Route 10 – Limehouse Basin and Limehouse Cut loop.
Route 13 – Isle of Dogs.

ROUTE INSTRUCTIONS:

1. A) Exit London Bridge station. Use the pedestrian crossing to turn right onto Tooley Street. Follow the cycle lane. Shortly past Potters Fields, take the left turn off the cycle path onto Queen Elizabeth Street. Turn left to pass over Tower Bridge. Dismount at the traffic lights and walk across the junction to your right. Keep heading right to St Katherine's Walk, which runs parallel to Tower Bridge Approach.

   B) Exit Fenchurch Street station and turn left onto Fenchurch Place. On the bend, walk your bike down the steps onto New London Street. Turn right at the T-junction onto Hart Road, which becomes Crutched Friars. Go straight on under the railway bridge. Take the right fork onto Crosswall. Pick up the cycle lane and make a compulsory right turn at the traffic lights onto Minories. This flows onto the busy multi-laned Goodman's Yard. Follow the cycle lane up to the traffic lights. Dismount and cross the junction to pick up the pavement cycle lane. Follow it under the railway bridge. When it ends, rejoin the road and continue along Mansell Street. At the next traffic lights dismount, walk towards Tower Bridge and onto St Katherine's Way.

2. At the bottom of the road, turn left under the Tower Hotel. Alternatively, dismount and continue straight down to the riverside path for stunning views of Tower Bridge. The path runs in front of the hotel before bending inland to rejoin the cycle route.

3. Cross over the red swing bridge passing St Katherine's Dock, where the road winds its way east past redeveloped warehouse accommodation. At the mini-roundabout go straight onto Wapping High Street. Take the immediate left onto Redmead Lane, through the yellow brick pillars onto the canal-side path of the Heritage Basin.

4. Follow the zigzag cycle path under the road, keeping to the left side of the canal. After passing the two ships of Tobacco Dock, the path rises up to cross Wapping Woods park before dropping back down to the canal-side again and entering Shadwell Basin.

5. Cycle around the perimeter of the dock to turn left onto Glamis Road. Take the immediate right down the path into King Edward Memorial Park. Follow the paved riverside path, passing Free Trade Wharf with its fantastic views of Docklands and Canary Wharf, for 500 metres, where the route bends away from the Thames and onto Narrow Street.

6. Follow the one-way system left onto Spert Street and Horseferry Road. Just before the road bends right, dismount and walk up to the Limehouse Basin along a short footpath next to a red and yellow brick building.

7. Return to Horseferry Road and follow the one-way system back to Narrow Street. Turn right. Once back to where the route emerged from the Thames Path, you have a choice: either retrace your route back to Tower Bridge or turn right (still on Narrow Road), making the route circular if less picturesque.

8. Turn left up to the dead end where you join the pavement, turning left to cross over the Limehouse Link (A1203) using the pelican

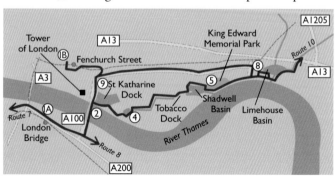

crossing. Turn left onto Butcher Row and then onto the contra-flow cycle lane on Cable Street. The route now veers west for 1.3 miles to Tower Bridge. The cycle lane is separate from the road and mostly has right of way, but take care with the roads that cross it.

9. After the traffic light junction with Dock Street, cross straight over into Royal Mint Street to continue on the cycle path.

10. At the junction with Mansell Street, turn left onto the pavement cycle path and then join the road. At the next traffic lights, dismount to walk towards Tower Bridge and back onto St Katherine's Way.

Distance: 7.25 miles. The route is ⅓ mile shorter if staying on the towpath.
Map: Ordnance Survey Explorer maps 162 and 173, and TfL Local Cycling Guide 7.
Surface and Gradients: The route consists of flat canal-side paths. It is generally paved or well-drained gravel, but can be muddy in a few places along the Lea Navigation section. Steps encountered to cross the A12 near Hackney Wick station and after crossing the Commercial Road A13.
Roads and road crossings: The major roundabout junction of the A12 and A11 is a return to urban traffic after the peaceful path along the River Lea Navigation. Dismount and take care, but the junctions are controlled by traffic lights so there are gaps in the traffic. Salmon Lane is a narrow high street with parked cars, so care is needed although it is only for 210 metres.
Refreshments: In Victoria Park there is the Pavilion Café and a water fountain. There are numerous pubs in the surrounding area, while the Limehouse Basin has three pubs with riverside views. Miller's House at Three Mills Island has a café open weekdays, and there are local shops on Salmon Lane.

This is a very pleasant ride along four different adjoining canals. It initially runs alongside Victoria Park and then follows Hertford Union Canal before turning south along the Regent's Canal. The route then dips into the Limehouse Basin before heading northeast up the Limehouse Cut. From there the route turns northwards up the River Lea Navigation, before returning again to the Hertford Union Canal to finish.

BACKGROUND AND PLACES OF INTEREST
Limehouse Basin and Limehouse Cut
The Limehouse Basin forms a link between the Thames and the Regent's Canal to the north and the Limehouse Cut to the northeast. Originally known as the Regent's Canal Dock on its opening in 1820, it was used to transfer cargo from seafaring ships to the barges of the canal. Once the railways started to dominate freight movement, the importance of the basin began to decline. It was not until 1968 that the basin was connected to the Limehouse Cut which was created in 1766, making it the oldest of the London canals. It created a short cut from the Thames at Limehouse, 2 miles northeast, to the Lea Navigation at Bow Locks. In 2003, an award-winning 240-metre section of floating towpath was created as a means to avoid the busy Blackwall Tunnel Northern Approach (A12), just before the locks.

Three Mills Island
Three Mills Island is a 35-acre site, part of the Lee Valley Regional Park. Behind the former distillery warehouses (now the new Three Mills Island film studios known for such TV programmes as Big Brother), there is the open space of Three Mills Green. House Mill is a Grade I listed building built in 1776 by Daniel Bisson, believed to be the largest tidal mill in the world; the adjacent Clock Mill, with its octagonal clock tower and oust houses, is a Grade II listed building built in 1817.

Starting Points & Transport:
1. Hackney Wick station – accessible via London Overground train services on the North London Line running between Richmond and Stratford.
2. Limehouse basin, if joining from Route 09.

Barges and boats in the Limehouse Basin, surrounded by revelopment.

3. The parking area around Victoria Park, exiting St Mark's Gate.
There is free street parking in the area north of the park. South of the park falls in
Tower Hamlets Zone B1, and so is only free on Sundays where allowed.

Links to other routes
Route 09 – Tower Bridge to Limehouse Basin loop.
Route 11 – Grand Union Canal: Regent's branch.
Route 17 – the River Lea Navigation.
Route 13 – Isle of Dogs.

ROUTE INSTRUCTIONS:
1. Exit Hackney Wick station, pass under the railway bridge and follow Wallis
Road to the T-junction with Chapman Road (A115). Cross straight over and
take the footbridge over the multi-lane East Cross Route (A12). Turn left onto
Cadogan Terrace then straight onto Wick Lane.

2. Turn left and walk down the ramp after the Top o' the Morning pub to join the
Hertford Union Canal. Turn right under the road bridge and pass the lock
before cycling again. This is Old Ford Middle Lock (No. 2), which climbs 2.7
metres and is unsafe for cycling.

3. After a further 125 metres dismount again as the road bridge and Old Ford Upper
Lock (No. 1), with its 1.9-metre climb, creates another unsafe section of towpath.*

4. Follow the canal parallel to Victoria Park before joining the Regent's Canal,
turning left and heading south. After passing under Roman Road (B119), either
take the well-signposted NCN 1 through Mile End Park (passing interesting
sculptures along the way) or follow the canal towpath.

5. From NCN 1 use the toucan crossing to Rhodeswell Road and rejoin the canal
again. After 300m (just before Salmon Lock), take the ramp up to Tomlin's
Terrace to join the road at a junction.

6. Go straight down Salmon Lane to pick up the cycle lane on the footpath at the
end. Use the toucan crossing to cross Commercial Road (A13). Turn sharp right
and go down the steps to the canal that feeds into the Limehouse Basin.

7. After exploring the Limehouse Basin, return back up the canal's sweeping bend
before it settles into a straight 2-mile run up to Bow Locks and Lea Navigation.
The towpath returns to gravel once clear of the basin. Just before Bow Locks,

take the new floating pontoon towpath to the left. Follow the green-edged path under the Blackwall Tunnel Northern Approach.

8. At Bow Locks, dismount to cross the footbridge. At Three Mills Island, cross the canal to travel up the opposite bank. The path is now large concrete slabs. As the canal path ends, turn left up to the main road. Note: there are plans for another new floating pontoon towpath, which will cut out instruction 9.

9. Dismount, turn right and follow the footpath up to the roundabout. Cross in a clockwise direction. On the other side of the flyover, look out for the path to the canal which starts where the railings end.

10. Slow down under bridges and around bends as visibility ahead is reduced. After the second bridge there are views of the magnificent Olympic Stadium in the distance. Just after a rail bridge the canal bends sharply, passing the closed old River Lea spur to reach Old Ford Lock. After the lock the path changes to a sealed surface, but it is frequently uneven in places.

11. Pass the Olympic site on your right and commercial properties on the opposite bank until the next bridge (White Post Lane, A115). Take the ramp up to the road, cross the canal and drop down to the opposite bank.

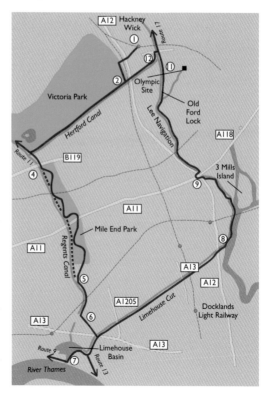

12. The towpath swings right and re-enters the Hertford Union Canal. Old Ford Lock No. 3 only climbs 1.1 metre and the path is wide, so it is easily ridden. The walls here are a popular site for graffiti art.

13. Just before Old Ford Lock No. 2, take the ramp up to Wick Lane. This is where the route first joined the canal. Backtrack to Hackney Wick station.

ROUTE 11
Grand Union Canal: Regent's Branch

Distance: 8.1 miles to Old Ford Lock (Victoria Park). Add 0.6 miles for ending at Hackney Wick station.

Map: Ordnance Survey Explorer map 173 and TfL Local Cycling Guide 7.

Surface and Gradients: The route is mainly on tarmac roads and sealed or paved towpaths. This is a flat ride where, apart from a slight hill in Islington the only gradients are ramps and bridges that connect the canal to roads. Steps are encountered getting down to the canal after Aberdeen Place in Maida Vale.

Roads and road crossings: Islington has some busy roads, but generally there is provision for cyclists or else walking the short distances is a possibility. The canal has narrow towpaths under bridges which, with the large number of pedestrians and cyclists, makes the 'Two Tings' rule vital.

Refreshments: Cafés in Sheldon Square, near Paddington Basin and Little Venice, and water taps along Lisson Grove Moorings. Divert from the route after London Zoo to visit two pubs on Princess Road (The Albert and The Engineer). Camden Lock Market has a diverse selection of world food stalls as well as restaurants and bars. Islington has many possibilities but there is also plenty of choice en route. The Constitution pub is actually accessed from the towpath, as is The Narrowboat, between City Road and Wenlock basins. Just after the Whitmore Road bridge at De Beauvoir Town is the Towpath Café – which is just that. Victoria Park has the Pavilion Café.

This route principally follows the Grand Union Canal's Regent's branch from Paddington to Old Ford Lock in Hackney. The Maida Hill tunnel and mile-long Islington tunnel both divert from the serenity of the canal to crest slight hills along roads that are thankfully light on traffic.

BACKGROUND AND PLACES OF INTEREST
Regent's Canal
Designed and constructed by John Nash and named after the Prince Regent of the time, this is part of the network across North London which links the Grand Union Canal's Paddington arm with East London's Limehouse Basin and docks. For a short time before the building of the railway network, it was the industrial transport system of London.

Starting Points & Transport:
1. Paddington station – accessible via Great Western services on the Greenford branch and to the west of London. There is no free street parking and strict permit zones. Use online sites to find private parking.
2. Hackney Wick station – accessible via London Overground train services on the North London Line running between Richmond and Stratford. There is free street parking in the area north of Victoria Park.

Links to other routes
Route 10 – Limehouse Basin and Limehouse Cut loop.
Route 12 – Grand Union Canal: Paddington Branch to Brentford Lock.
Route 17 – The River Lea Navigation.
Route 21 – Regent's Park to Hampstead Heath.

ROUTE INSTRUCTIONS:
1. To exit Paddington station, take the lift next to Platform 1 up to the bridge. Turn left out of the exit, taking the footpath. Cyclists must walk this first section, passing under the flyover before emerging next to the canal.

2. Before going under the next road bridge (Westway, A40), turn right to cross the canal on the silver-ramped footbridge. It is worth taking a short diversion up to the Little Venice Canal Basin; don't cross the footbridge but continue under the A40 and Harrow Road (A404) bridges.

3. Once over the canal turn sharp right and then left into the bright orange and yellow subway. Turn left out of the subway up a shared path (Little Venice Walk). To carry on along Warwick Avenue, dismount and use the zebra crossings.

4. Cross the bridge over the Regent's Canal before the busy crossroads complicates the right turn into Blomfield Road. Care is needed but traffic lights help.

5. Cross straight over Edgware Road (A5) onto a cycle lane leading onto Aberdeen Place. Dismount and walk down the alleyway where the road bends left. Take the steps down to ride along the canal towpath. Dismount to pass through the 48-metre Eyre's Tunnel (under Lisson Grove, B507), which goes straight into another section where walking is essential. This is the Lisson Grove Moorings, otherwise known as Marylebone Wide. Cycle past rail and road bridges, and along the picturesque section around Regent's Park.

6. Macclesfield Bridge (B525, left), about midway on the Regent's Park section, commonly known as 'Blow-Up Bridge'. (The first bridge was destroyed by an explosion in 1874.)

7. Pass the great aviary in the Zoological Gardens. The towpath bends sharply left at a small basin, passing under the Prince Albert Road bridge and heading north towards Camden.

8. To get to the pubs on Princes Road, leave the canal via the ramp where the road and rail bridges are very close together.

St Pancras Lock, with a barge in the background.

9. Look out for graffiti by mysterious artist Banksy as the route approaches Camden Lock (actual name Hampstead Road Lock). Walk around the Dingwall's basin, entering just before the black and white footbridge over the canal. Rejoin the path next to the lock until past the road bridge (Camden High Street, A502) before cycling. Pass Hawley Lock and Kentish Town Lock. The Constitution pub's canal-side entrance is after the fifth bridge (St Pancras Way).

Graffiti under the Oval Road bridge by the infamous Banksy, with additions by disgruntled peers.

10. The next canal features are St Pancras Basin and St Pancras Lock, after which the distinctive King's Cross gasholder can be seen in the distance. The canal passes under two more bridges (the second is York Way, A5200) and Battlesbridge basin. After passing under the Caledonian Road (A5203) bridge, the route leaves the canal where it enters the Islington Tunnel.

11. Climb the steep ramp onto Muriel Street. There are signs for 'Regent's Canal bypass' along the next section. Turn right uphill along Carnegie Street. Turn left to Charlotte Terrace and right again onto Copenhagen Street. Pick up the cycle lane and continue straight ahead until the five-road junction. Turn right onto Cloudesley Road, passing through the gap for cyclists. Take the second left up Richie Street and continue over Liverpool Road. At the end of Bromfield Street, where only cyclists can get through, turn left onto Parkfield Street and follow around onto Berners Road, coming out next to the Business Design Centre.

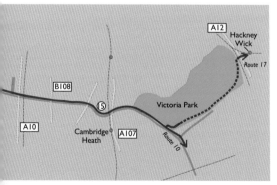

12. Cautious cyclists can dismount and use the pedestrian crossing to turn right and then walk up Carlton Place to Colebrooke Row (140 metres). Otherwise, turn left and take the first right up to Islington Green (A104). Take the first right and then the first right again down Colebrooke Row.

13. Take the first left into Gerrard Road followed by a right turn onto Danbury Street. After 70 metres turn left to join the canal again.

14. Pass City Road Lock and City Road basin, the largest of the Regent's Canal basins. Just after the Wharf Road bridge and adjacent Narrowboat pub, the smaller Wenlock basin can be seen on the opposite side of the canal. Sturt's Lock is 350 metres further on. About 700 metres/the third bridge from Sturt's Lock is a canal-side café and bicycle repair shop. The towpath goes over a humped-back bridge at the entrance to Kingsland basin. Look across the canal to see the sign for Shoreditch on the waterline. Pass under the Kingsland Road bridge (A10) and the London Overground Line rail bridge. After 880 metres you will reach Acton's Lock. The cycle shop/café Lock Seven is on the opposite bank.

15. Pass under two more bridges (including Cambridge Heath's bridge, A107) before the start of Victoria Park. After 550 metres you will reach Old Ford Lock. Turn left into Victoria Park. Exit via the perimeter road to Cadogan Gate and follow the signs to Hackney Wick station.

The Paddington branch of the Grand Union Canal passes through the Northolt & Greenford Country Park with a footbridge leading to Northala Fields.

Distance: 26.2 miles.

Map: Ordnance Survey Explorer map 173 and TfL Local Cycling Guides 6 and 7.

Surface and Gradients: This is a flat route with a gentle drop down from Hanwell Locks to Osterley, or an incline if the route is done in reverse. A few sections are inclined to be muddy or rutted under bridges, so a mountain bike with knobbly tyres is recommended but not essential. Steps are encountered to reach the A40 cyclepath.

Roads and road crossings: There is a short section on the road just after Bulls Bridge and finally from Great Western Road to Orchard Road, but this could be walked.

Refreshments: Much of the route is limited to the towpath where access to refreshments is not always easy, so make sure you have topped up your water bottle. The Waterside Café on Little Venice is accessible, as is Jake's Cabin Café near Acton Lane Bridge. There are also a few pubs on the route: The Grand Junction Arms (Acton Lane), The Pleasure Boat (Alperton), and The Black Horse (Greenford), which has a beer garden next to the canal.

A barge at Little Venice.

This route follows the Grand Union Canal from the inner city out to the big industrial zones and the outlying areas of the capital. Finally, the route dips into the countryside before returning to Brentford.

BACKGROUND AND PLACES OF INTEREST

Grand Junction Canal

The works on the main Grand Union Canal between Brentford and Braunston began in 1793. The Paddington branch of the canal was started two years later. The project produced a 13½-mile lock-free canal acclaimed at the time as a 'great liquid road'. When the Grand Junction Canal Company opened the Paddington branch on 10th July 1801, it was claimed 20,000 people lined the canal for miles. In 1929 the Regent's Canal and Grand Junction Canal merged to form the Grand Union Canal.

Starting Points & Transport:

1. Paddington station – accessible via Great Western services on the Greenford branch and to the west of London.
2. Kensal Rise station or Kensal Green station – accessible via London Overground services on the North London Line running between Richmond and Stratford. Kensal Green also served by Bakerloo Line. No free street parking.
3. Brentford – accessible via South West Trains services on the Hounslow Loop Line between Waterloo and Richmond. Anglia Railways services on London Cross Link between Norwich and Basingstoke.

Links to other routes

Route 03 – Richmond Lock to Richmond via Kew Bridge.
Route 04 – Barnes Bridge to Kew Bridge loop is nearby (use route 03 for details).
Route 11 – Grand Union Canal: Regent's Branch.
Route 20 – Hyde Park and The Mall.

ROUTE INSTRUCTIONS:

1. To exit Paddington station, take the lift next to Platform 1 up to the bridge. Turn left out of the exit, taking the footpath. Cyclists must walk this first section, passing under the flyover before emerging next to the canal. Start cycling here, following the canal straight ahead towards the picturesque Little Venice basin.

2. On passing the Waterside Café leave the towpath. At the top of the ramp cross straight over to Delamare Terrace. Do not be tempted to cycle under the bridge as the towpath here is too narrow. As the road bends to the left, drop down the bank on the cycle lane, passing between St Mary Magdalene Church and the canal. After 230 metres, pass through the gate to rejoin the towpath. Dismount for the very narrow path under the Harrow Road bridge. Now you can cycle for the rest of the route! After the next bridge (Great Western Road), pass Meanwhile Gardens where NCN Route 06 currently starts.

3. After the next road bridge (Ladbroke Grove), enter Kensal basin with Kensal Green cemetery on the opposite bank.

4. There is a road bridge (Scrubs Lane) and then a rail bridge.

5. Pass under two more rail bridges and a road bridge (Old Oak Lane).

6. The path bends to the left, passing under two rail bridges and changing back to a sealed path. After a third of a mile, pass under the next road bridge (Acton Lane).

7. After passing under the next road bridge (Abbey Road), the canal bends right before it crosses the North Circular (A406).

8. After one more rail and road bridge (Ealing Road, A4005), you will pass through Alperton. There is a pub (The Pleasure Boat) just over the bridge on the left.

9. Pass under Manor Farm Road bridge and enter the open countryside surrounding Sudbury and Horsenden Hill to the north. The path here changes to gravel and becomes narrower, so take extra care and slow down for pedestrians. There is a kissing gate just before the only original bridge (Horsenden Lane) left en route along the Paddington branch. Beware the very narrow path under the bridge.

10. After one more bridge (Greenford Road, A4127) and kissing gate, you return to the industrial area around Greenford. The canal turns sharply left and passes under another Oldfield Lane bridge before opening up to allow boat turning.

11. Heading southwards, the path narrows and deteriorates a little. After passing under Auriol Drive, the towpath passes over its own bridge. Slightly further, pass under the iron bridge for the Central Line. Non-mountain bike riders may need to walk under this bridge as it is particularly rutted.

12. NCN Route 6 leaves the canal 0.6 miles later via the next footbridge. The Mohammedi Park Masjid Complex can be seen opposite bank.

13. Pass under the huge A40 road bridge (Western Avenue) and enter open countryside. You could use the wooden footbridge for a trip to Northala Fields.

14. Pass under two more bridges (Kensington Road and Ruislip Road) before a short return to light industry on the opposite bank. Pass the Engineers Wharf moorings on the opposite bank – behind which is Grand Union Village, the recently built apartment block development on the brownfield site of an aggregates storage depot. There is an option here to take the next footbridge to visit Willowtree Marina.

15. After a brief return to suburbia at the next road bridge (Uxbridge Road, A4020), this is the remotest stretch of the route. The canal here forms the boundary between Hayes and Southall. The path becomes quite bumpy and sections stay damp even in the summer. Pass under the vast 5-track rail bridge on a slight bend in the canal and yet another kissing gate as you approach Bulls Bridge.

Alperton.

16. At the Bulls Bridge Junction, turn left onto a much wider sealed path to leave the Paddington branch and join the Grand Union Canal's main line.

17. Head east away from the canal, down Bulls Bridge Road away for just under half a mile, passing the Grand Junction Arms pub. Due to a blind spot at the junction, turn left down Western Road and use the mini-roundabout to return to make a safe left turn into The Common. Pass The Old Oak pub. Turn left into Regina Road. Cross over the green on the right to rejoin the canal in the far corner.

18. The gravel path is perfectly straight until Norwood Top Lock. Half a mile from rejoining the path, it crosses a side arm of the canal via a narrow bridge and then passes under a road bridge (Norwood Road, A3005).

19. After half a mile there is another steep side-arm crossing bridge followed closely by Norwood Top Lock, the first of 11 locks between here and Brentford basin. The next road bridge (Windmill Lane, A4127) is a viaduct over a railway (the freight line from Southall to Brentford).

20. Enter the impressive series of six locks which forms the Hanwell Flight. The lock system runs adjacent to the yellow-brick Ealing Hospital, originally known as County Asylum; the second lock was consequently known as Asylum Lock. British Waterways ask cyclists to walk through the Hanwell Flight.

21. Pass under the road bridge (Trumpers Way, A3005) and enter the River Brent Nature Reserve of reclaimed meadows, scrubland and associated birdlife. Pass Osterley Lock and under the girder road bridge of the M4 motorway to the Piccadilly Line rail bridge. The towpath changes sides for the first time over Gallows Bridge. From here the route leaves the countryside and re-enters urbanisation. Pass Clitheroe's Lock.

22. To get to Brentford station, take the steps up to the busy Great Western Road (A4) and use the cycle lane on the pavement. Take care where the path diverts around the GSK (Glaxo Smithkline) entrance. At the next traffic lights, dismount and turn right to Boston Manor Road (A3002). Take the first left down Orchard Road and straight on to the station.

23. To continue to Brentford Lock, pass under the Great Western Road (A4) bridge and a rail bridge, taking the towpath that passes a warehouse building covering a canal basin. Emerge along the Brentford Marina at Brentford Lock. Route 03 – Richmond Lock to Richmond via Kew Bridge (including Syon House) – is joined from here.

ROUTE 13
The Isle of Dogs

Distance: 4.3 miles on the Isle of Dogs using 4(a). Add 640 metres if using 4(b).
Map: Ordnance Survey Explorer map 162 and TfL Local Cycling Guide 7.
Surface and Gradients: This is a flat ride on sealed roads and paths. Trafalgar Way is the only exception, where there is a slight hill. Sometimes the Greenwich Foot Tunnel lifts are not working, so cyclists must be prepared to carry their bikes up or down the 100-odd stairs on each side. Steps are encountered going up to the Cartier Circle roundabout if using 4(a) and to cross South Dock.
Roads and road crossings: Westferry Road, Manchester Road and Prestons Road can all be busy at times, but generally feel safe. Between Admirals Way and Mastmaker Road traffic can be intimidating, so consider crossing on foot.
Refreshments: Greenwich has an abundance of refreshment facilities. Island Gardens (where the Greenwich Foot Tunnel's northern entrance is situated) has a small café but no toilets. The Gun pub in Cold Harbour is worth saving until the end of the ride, where a riverside drink or a meal can be enjoyed while watching the changing light on the Millennium Dome/O2 Arena across the water. The Ferry House Pub, off Ferry Road, is said to be the oldest pub on the Isle of Dogs.

The Isle of Dogs is dominated by high-rise buildings; This route is very quiet on a Sunday or bank holiday.

BACKGROUND AND PLACES OF INTEREST

The Isle of Dogs' northern boundary is the East India Dock Road (A13), The peninsula was originally known as Stepney Marsh. The docks were part of the Port of London, once the world's largest port. The first to be built were West India Docks between 1799 and 1806. Situated further south, the Millwall Dock was opened in 1868. The spoil formed the area known as the Mudchute. After terrible bombing during World War II, the docks thrived for 25 years, but then rapidly declined and shut down in 1980.

Starting Points & Transport:

1. Greenwich station – accessible via South Eastern services on the London Cannon Street to Slade Green Line. Also services from London Bridge, Charing Cross and Waterloo East stations. (Bikes are not allowed on the DLR.)
2. Greenwich Foot Tunnel.
3. Greenwich Council runs car parks in Cutty Sark Gardens, SE10, and also in Burney Street, SE10 – £1 per hour, no time limit. Underground car park in Canada Wharf Car Park, E14 5EQ.

Links to other routes:

Route 08 – Tower Bridge to Greenwich.
Route 09 – Tower Bridge to Limehouse Basin loop.
Route 10 – Limehouse Basin and Limehouse Cut loop.
Route 16 – The Waterlink Way.

Entrance to The Greenwich Tunnel, Island Gardens.

ROUTE INSTRUCTIONS:

1. A) Exit Greenwich Station. Confident riders can turn left onto Greenwich High Road (A206) and continue to the one-way system. Take the right fork into Greenwich Church Street leading to the Cutty Sark and Greenwich Foot Tunnel.

   B) For a quieter but longer route, exit the station from Platform 1 using the ramp to Tarves Way. Turn right onto the path that feeds into Straightmouth. At the fork in the road turn left along Randall Place. Turn right after the school onto Haddo Street. Pass around the barrier and continue to the junction with Creek Road. Cross into Norway Street,

From the South Docks drawbridge, looking east at the Millennium Dome/O² Arena.

turn right onto Thames Street, then take a left up Horseferry Place. Continue to the Thames riverside and turn right to reach the Cutty Sark and the Greenwich Foot Tunnel entrance.

2. Exit the northern entrance of the foot tunnel into Island Gardens Park and follow the path along the riverside and continue until forced inland by Newcastle Draw Dock.

3. Turn right and join Saunders Ness Road, then turn left onto Seyssel Street after the school. Turn right onto Manchester Road or dismount and use the zebra crossing to the left. Continue to the roundabout and carry straight on to Prestons Road, to cross the drawbridge entrance to South Dock.

4. There are two options for the next section:
   A) For the quieter route: take the first left after the bridge, leading to Wood Wharf Business Park and passing three cranes. The road bends sharp right by a huge satellite dish. On the next sharp bend (to the left), leave the road and join a path running straight ahead to the Cartier Circle roundabout, via the steps.
   B) For a busier route with no steps: use the bus lane at Prestons Road before leaving the road to join the shared path (where the Blackwall basin joins the Thames). Turn left and left again at the next roundabout, then leave the shared path to join Trafalgar Way leading to the Cartier Circle roundabout.

5. Leave the roundabout on Churchill Place and follow the one-way system for a circuit of Canary Wharf, firstly along South Colonnade. Turn right around Cabot Square and then just after joining North Colonnade dismount and walk between the buildings on the left to cross the footbridge to West India Quay for Docklands Museum. Return to continue along North Colonnade.

6. Rejoin South Colonnade but turn left at the second set of traffic lights onto Upper Bank Street. Pass Jubilee Park on the right. Dismount and go down the steps to South Dock. Turn right and take the footbridge over the dock. On the other side, turn left and then right onto Admirals Way to cycle again. Pass under the DLR and turn right onto Marsh Wall, followed by a left turn into Mastmaker Road. The route is now on NCN 1. Follow the road to the left into Lightermans Road.

7. Turn right onto Millharbour. After 270 metres turn left off the road into a pedestrian shopping area (Pepper Street). Cross the drawbridge over Millwall Inner Dock. Turn right and follow the path along the dockside until the park. Take the curved path away from the dock and under the DLR, before it meets the zigzag ramp up to East Ferry Road.

8. Turn right and continue straight ahead (leaving NCN 1), crossing the give way lines onto Ferry Street. After the Ferry House pub, turn right and then left to follow along the Thames, eventually joining Napier Ave. Turn right opposite the Masthouse Terrace Pier.

9. At the crossroads, turn left onto Westferry Road (A1206). Continue for 620 metres, passing the old Limehouse Reach entrance to Millwall Dock.

10. Turn left onto Arnhem Place and continue onto the riverside. Follow the path right, passing Sir John McDougal Gardens and continuing all the way to South Dock Entrance where the path bends inland.

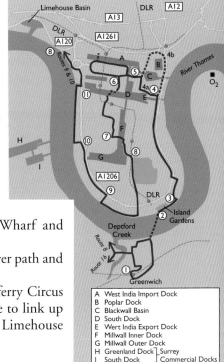

11. Turn left to join Westferry Road and carry straight on at the Heron Quays roundabout with the traffic light sculpture. Switch to the right lane to climb up to the top of Westferry Circus. Cautious riders can dismount and walk across to the central reservation. The route ends with a lap of Westferry Circus Gardens. From here there is a choice of route[s] back to the Greenwich Foot Tunnel:
(a) West India Avenue through Canary Wharf and the footbridge across South Dock, Pepper Street and Millwall Inner Dock.
(b) West India Avenue through Canary Wharf and continue down Prestons Road.
(c) Return along the last section along the river path and Westferry Road.
Riders can walk down the steps from Westferry Circus towards the Thames along Canary Riverside to link up with the Limehouse Basin (Route 09) and Limehouse Cut loop (Route 10).

A	West India Import Dock
B	Poplar Dock
C	Blackwall Basin
D	South Dock
E	West India Export Dock
F	Millwall Inner Dock
G	Millwall Outer Dock
H	Greenland Dock ⎤ Surrey
I	South Dock ⎦ Commercial Docks

ROUTE 14
Coulsdon to Hackbridge via Mitcham Common
(The Wandle Trail: Part One)

Distance: The whole route ending at Hackbridge Station is 11.5 miles. If finishing at Mitcham Junction Station the route is 8.25 miles.

Map: Ordnance Survey Explorer maps 146 and 161, and TfL Local Cycling Guides 10 and 12.

Surface and Gradients: After a gradual uphill start there is a very steep climb of 138 feet over ¾ of a mile, but once at the top the ride falls all the way down to Mitcham Common. The route is predominantly roads and tarmac paths. Steps are encountered using the footbridge over the rail tracks near Mitcham Common. Mitcham gravel beds section has a few muddy places after wet weather.

Roads and road crossings: For the short section until the route joins Chipstead Valley Road, traffic can be busy. Between Oaks Park and the Oaks track traffic can travel fast. From the Wandle River to Mitcham Common, less confident riders may be better off walking short sections; the same is true from Beddington Park to Hackbridge Station.

Refreshments: There are several good pubs along the route and the Oaks Park has a good tearoom with seating outside. Beddington Park has a café open 7 days a week.

This is the first of two routes following sections of the Wandle Trail, picking it up in Carshalton and leaving it between Mitcham and Hackbridge. This is a path that follows the Wandle River to its confluence with the Thames in Wandsworth. After leaving the trail to cross Mitcham Common, the route passes through Beddington Park and ends at Hackbridge Station via gravel abstraction pits and a nature reserve.

BACKGROUND AND PLACES OF INTEREST

Mayflower Lavender Fields

In summer you could be forgiven for thinking you were in the South of France. 'The home of English Lavender', the 25-acre farm sits in the heart of what was once the most prolific lavender-growing area in the world.

Oaks Park

This is a magnificent landscaped park with a variety of facilities. Once through the woodland screen, there are fantastic views stretching towards the cityscape of London. The Earl of Derby laid out the park in the 1770s in the fashionable landscape style. In the latter half of the 19th century it was bisected by a tree-lined drive. This is now used as a car park.

Starting Points & Transport:

1. Coulsdon South station – accessible via Southern Railways services from Charing Cross and London Bridge. There are only trains via Victoria on Sundays, but they go via Clapham Junction.
2. Woodmansterne station – accessible via Southern Railways services from London Bridge via East Croydon.
3. By car: Lion Green Road car park in Coulsdon. (A little way up Chipstead Valley Road there is free kerbside parking.
4. Hackbridge station – accessible via First Capital Connect services on Sutton Loop and Southern services on Sutton & Mole Valley Lines out of Victoria.
5. Mitcham Junction station – accessible via South Eastern services on West Croydon to Wimbledon Line. Also all of the services listed above for Hackbridge.

Links to other routes

Route 15 – Mitcham Common to Wandsworth (The Wandle Trail: Part Two).

The Oaks Track heading uphill through the countryside.

ROUTE INSTRUCTIONS:

1. A) Walk out of Coulsdon South Station and turn right over the pelican crossing to the busy A237. Pass under the railway bridge and adjoining flyover where the shared path starts. Follow the embankment signposted 'Coulsdon Town Centre'. Turn right up the wooded lane and left onto the busy Lion Green Road.
B) Exit the Lion Green Road car park, turning left.
C) Head south down Woodstock Road. Turn right at the T-Junction with Chipstead Valley Road.

2. Turn left at the traffic lights onto Chipstead Valley Road.
A) Continue for about 1 mile to the right then turn onto Rectory Lane. Fit riders may continue up this winding road with no pavement for the ¾ mile to the top and then turn right onto Carshalton Road.
B) Slower riders can take the second left into Manor Way, then turn right at the crossroads for the slog up Chipstead Way. At the top turn right onto Woodmansterne Street and first left to rejoin the route on Carshalton Road. This detour only adds 90 metres to the route.

3. Descend to the junction with Croydon Lane (A2022). Mayfield lavender fields are on the left. Turn left, taking the path adjacent to the road, and use the Pegasus crossing to enter Oaks Park through the black metal gate. Pass the Oaks Park Tearooms, following the road signposted NCN 20 to the right. The road becomes sandy as it runs downhill.

4. At the bottom, take care when turning right onto the fast-moving Woodmansterne Road. Take the immediate left up Oaks Track, which is signposted as a dead-end. There is now a refreshing uphill ride through open countryside. After passing the gate, continue straight ahead until turning left at the crossroads.

5. The route eventually rejoins suburbia and sealed roads on a bend. Go straight onto Boundary Road for the 0.6 mile-run downhill to the junction with Stanley Park Road. There is a special cycle crossing on the left. Follow the cycle lane back onto Boundary Road, which becomes Park Lane after crossing the railway lines.

The view of the Wandle from the Nightingale Road bridge.

One of the many specially designed bridges by Andrew Sabin along the Wandle Trail.

6. Proceed straight on for about ¾ mile until the T-junction with Acre Lane. Leave the road to take the cycle lane around to the toucan crossing and proceed down Westcroft Road. Continue straight as the road winds its way to the Westcroft Leisure Centre. Enter the car park, follow its one-way system and pick up the shared path in the far right-hand corner.

7. Watch carefully for the white cyclist symbol and the number 20 painted on the road in order to negotiate Parksfield Close, turn left onto Devonshire Road and then right into Lakesview Close. Cross the car park and turn right to join the cycle path, which leads to a little bridge over a stream – the mighty Wandle!

8. Turn right and follow the path, which leads to Mill Lane. Continue under the railway bridge, keeping the wooded area on your right. Look out for the entrance to Wilderness Island on the right, opposite Strawberry Lane.

9. After the road bends sharply to the left, look out for the tarmac path on your right which leads into the wooded area. This is the start of many miles of following the Wandle north. After 400 yards the path bends away from the river.

10. Turn right to take the path up to Nightingale Road. Turn right, signposted for NCN 20 to Morden and Colliers Wood. Follow the cycle lane that takes you over the Wandle and ends where you turn left, following the NCN sign back to the Wandle river path. Follow the path behind the blocks of flats.

11. Take care crossing Culvers Avenue. On the other side of the road is a cycle-friendly kissing gate. The path carries on between the river and the backs of houses. Look out for the left-hand fork as it bends away from the river. Cross the river on a spiral bridge (No. 86). Turn right and carry on along the opposite bank. Use the pelican crossing to cross Middleton Road.

12. Turn immediate left into Watermead Lane if continuing north to Wandsworth following Route 15. Otherwise carry on along Middleton Road, which becomes

Goat Road and leads up to the mini one-way system at the Carshalton Road junction. Turn left. The road is busy here, so consider walking on the pavement or on the path in front of the houses. Take Drakes Road back onto the Carshalton Road and turn left on the pavement cycle path.

13. A) To end the ride at Mitcham Junction station, use the second pelican crossing. B) To continue south to Beddington Park, use the first pelican crossing and turn right, doubling back on yourself for about 30 yards and looking out for the black metal barrier on the left. Take the sandy path across the common which arcs to the right where it enters the trees, ending next to the railway lines. Take the footbridge over the lines and turn right, pass through the gate and head south parallel to the railway tracks. Enjoy the open space between here and Beddington Park.

14. Pass through the kissing gate and the wooded fringe of the park. Turn left, taking the sealed path. Follow past the football pitches. (The left turn next to the children's playground leads to a café.) To explore the park further, pass over the Wandle via the ornate bridge. Emerge next to the East Lodge gatehouse and turn right. Just after St Mary's Church on the left and the double-arched cemetery gate on the right, turn right onto a shared cycle path by the white barrier gate. Go straight and take the left-hand fork where a footpath splits off to the right. Keep going straight all the way to the car park.

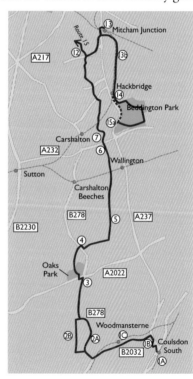

15. A) The more confident rider can exit the park here, turning right onto the very busy London Road for the two thirds of a mile to Hackbridge Station.
B) Alternatively, turn around and retrace the route back through the park, passing the café and onto the gravel pits entrance. Continue straight onto the London Road. This will avoid as much of the road as possible but will add 0.85 miles to the route.

16. Turn right. There is no cycle lane or path so you may choose to wheel your bike for the last ¼ mile. At present there is no pelican crossing, so take care.

Distance: 8.45 miles starting from Mitcham Junction station. 8.8 miles starting from Hackbridge station.

Map: Ordnance Survey Explorer map 161 and TfL Local Cycling Guide 10.

Surface and Gradients: A flat riverside path with some roads. Most paths are tarmac but a few are hard-packed gravel.

Roads and road crossings: Bishopsford Road/London Road (A217) must be crossed with care. The Croydon Tramlink is just after Morden Hall Park; it is essential to look both ways, as the trams are quiet and move very fast. The section on Garratt Lane (A217), near Earlsfield station, is busy with no cycle lane, but it only lasts for 180 metres so it can be walked. After King George's Park, the route returns to Garratt Lane and the busy Wandsworth area. Cyclists may wish to double back to end at Earlsfield station.

Refreshments: Morden Hall is a National Trust property which includes the Snuff Mill Café. Merton Abbey Mills has plenty to choose. Deen City Farm's café is open Tuesday to Sunday. There is a large superstore at Merantun Way, Colliers Wood, which has toilets and a restaurant. Garratts Lane, Earlsfield has reasonable cafés, while Wandsworth Town station is near a pub and restaurant.

This route follows the remainder of the well-signposted NCN 20 and the Wandle Trail, from Mitcham down to its confluence with the Thames at Bell Creek, Wandsworth. It is a very pleasant riverside path for most of the ride, but gets a little bleak approaching the Thames. At some points the cycling and walking routes of the Wandle Trail differ slightly, so rely on the NCN 20 signs.

BACKGROUND AND PLACES OF INTEREST
Morden Hall Park
Built in 1770, Morden Hall Park has at different times been a family home, a boarding school for young gentlemen and a military hospital during the First World War. The park is on the flood plain of the River Wandle and includes meadows, marshland, woodland, wetlands and waterways, as well as a formal rose garden. There is a riverside café, gift shop and second-hand bookshop in the old walled kitchen garden.

Deen City Farm
Based on National Trust land on the fringes of the South Wimbledon Business Area, this is a unique educational resource and is open to the public six days a week (closed on Monday) for farm tours – admission is free. The gardens include an orchard/wildlife area, a pond, vegetable and flower growing areas, a giant nature search, a composting area, a grassed picnic area, a maze and an eco cob building.

Merton Abbey Mills
This craft village is housed in a former textiles factory. In 1881 it was acquired by textile designer William Morris as the new home of Morris & Co.'s workshops. Liberty & Co. were also involved with the site from the 19th century, and took over the facilities in 1940. (Their popular ranges of fabrics were made there up until 1972.) The craft village now hosts a weekend market, with indoor and outdoor stalls selling a range of hand-crafted goods.

Morden Hall Park.

Starting Points & Transport:

1. Hackbridge station – accessible via First Capital Connect services on the Sutton loop and Southern services on Sutton & Mole Valley lines out of Victoria. Parking at £4.10 per day.
2. Mitcham Junction station – accessible via Network Southeast Services on the West Croydon to Wimbledon line, and all of the services listed above for Hackbridge.

If continuing from Route 14, start from (3). If starting from Mitcham Junction, start route instructions from (2).

The route crosses the Tramlink. Look both ways, as the trams make very little noise.

Links to other routes

Route 06 – Battersea to Putney Bridge via Chelsea Harbour.
Route 14 – Coulsdon to Hackbridge via Mitcham Common.

ROUTE INSTRUCTIONS:

1. Exit Hackbridge station and cross the busy London Road into the one-way street entering the Felnex Trading Estate. Take the first right. Turn left onto Hackbridge Road where there is no cycle lane as such, but there are painted cyclist logos at intervals. As the road bends to the left over the Wandle River, the cycle path entrance is signposted on the opposite side. Take care crossing Culvers Avenue and follow the path beside the river, behind the blocks of flats. Look out for the left-hand fork as the path bends away from the river. Cross over a spiral bridge. Turn right and carry on along the opposite bank. Take the pelican crossing to Middleton Road. Turn immediately left into Watermead Lane. Go to (3).

2. Exit Mitcham Junction station left. Use the pelican crossing over the busy Carshalton Road to join the cycle lane on the opposite footpath. Turn right into Drakes Lane. Turn left along the path that runs in front of the houses. Cross Arney's Lane and continue. On reaching Goat Lane, dismount and walk the short distance past the Goat pub. Once clear of the one-way section, turn right onto Goat Lane. Continue ahead for about a third of a mile.

3. After the bridge over the Wandle, use the pelican crossing to turn right into Watermead Lane. At the end, go through the kissing gate that's just big enough for bikes, where the tarmac path becomes narrow and bumpy. After 0.36 miles the river bends around to the right as the path diverges left and rises, before levelling out to join a road. Keep going straight towards Bishopsford Road/London Road (A217). Note: Sustrans wish to develop this section of the route, so it may change in the future.

4. Turn right to cross this busy road. (It may be safer to turn left first and use the central refuge.) After the petrol station on the left the footpath widens, leading to the footbridge over the Wandle. The path turns back on itself as it rejoins the river. Pass through Ravensbury Park, staying on the right bank. Pass a Sustrans marker

Millstone monument near Ravensbury Park Weir.

showing 5 miles to Wandsworth. Pass to the right of the millstone monument next to Ravensbury Park Weir and emerge through the kissing gate onto a service road adjacent to Morden Road (A239).

5. Follow the signs to Morden Hall Park. Use the toucan crossing to turn right onto the cycle lane. Turn left into the park just after the bus stop. Take the gravel path down the avenues of trees. The river is crossed 5 times within the park. Follow the signs for the Wandle Trail which lead out of the park to the Tramlink crossing. Pass Deen City Farm before crossing Windsor Avenue and reaching Merton Abbey Mills, on the right just before the toucan crossing over Merantun Way (A24).

6. Go through the arch to cross Station Road before rejoining the wide path on the left bank of the Wandle. The route now follows an intricate section through residential streets. Cross Merton High Street into Holmes Road via the toucan crossing and follow until turning right at the T-junction into Laburnam Road, which becomes Hanover Road. Turn right onto All Saints Road and left onto East Road. At the mini-roundabout turn right onto North Road. Just after Wandle Meadows Nature Park turn left into Mead Path. Turn left at the right-hand bend to join the path under the railway bridge. The river on the left is now Norbury Brook but on the next bend it joins the Wandle.

7. After another 400 metres use the toucan crossing over Plough Lane and rejoin the Wandle on the opposite bank. The path passes through the Lower Wandle Nature Reserve before reaching the Trewint Street Bridge 0.75 miles later. Turn right over the bridge. At the crossroads turn left, taking the contra-flow cycle lane into Summerley Street.

8. Turn left at the T-junction with Garratts Lane. After 180 metres turn left onto the quieter Penwith Road. Take the first left into Ravensbury Terrace, then turn right into Ravensbury Road and right into Acuba Road. Continue for 200 metres until the road bends left but the path continues straight into King George's Park. For

half a mile follow the clearly defined path across the park. Cross over Kimber Road and back into the park again for 550 metres towards the distant tower block.

9. Turn right to leave the park onto Mapleton Road and continue to the T-junction with Garratt Lane. Take a glance over the bridge at the Wandle before it disappears for a while. Turn left on the cycle lane up to the crossroads with Wandsworth High Street (A3). Cross over at the traffic lights into Ram Street and along the red bus and cycle lane, passing the Young's brewery on the left. The top of Ram Street forks right but the cycle route takes you to the triangular pedestrian island. Use the toucan crossing to turn left onto the pavement cycle path at Armoury Way.

10. After 140 metres, pass the blue and yellow bridge over the Wandle again. Turn sharp right in front of the Crane pub onto Dormay Street and straight back up The Causeway. Be very careful, as the industrial traffic may not expect a bike coming in the opposite direction. On the next slight bend in the road the Wandle is split. On the right there is an unusual sluice gate with a bell and the inscription, 'I am rung by the tides.' Pass under the low railway bridge.

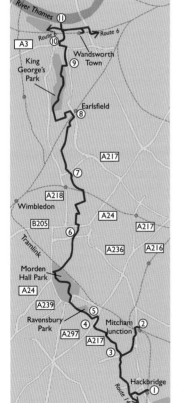

11. The road ends next to a large featureless building. Cross over the path (London Network 37) and down the decking onto The Spit. There is a pyramidal sculpture on the end.

12. Return to Route 37 and turn right towards Enterprise Way. Turn right again, following the path up the west side of Bell Creek to the Thames itself. This section of the path is in a development area and is only opened at the owner's discretion, so it may be shut.

13. A) To get to Wandsworth Town: go back down Route 37 but carry on past The Spit on the left. Continue straight onto Smugglers Way. This road becomes busier as it approaches a major junction with Swandon Way (A217). Just after Marl Road, take the skinny central bike lane which has its own traffic light to aid safe crossing. Continue around the bend and under the railway bridge to Wandsworth Town station.

B) To get to Putney: see Route 06 – Battersea to Putney Bridge via Chelsea Harbour – for more details.

ROUTE 16
The Waterlink Way

Ladywell Fields

Distance: 9.9 miles.

Map: Ordnance Survey Explorer map 161 and TfL Local Cycling Guides 7 and 10.

Surface and Gradients: The route crosses a generally flat river-plain ride that climbs 95 feet over about 10 miles, mainly on sealed roads and paths. Within South Norwood County Park, there are well-drained hard-packed gravel paths.

Roads and road crossings: There is some unavoidable heavy traffic around Greenwich at the start. Creek Road is short but unsympathetic to cycling. There is little provision for cycling at the right turn into Ladywell Fields Park on Ladywell Road (B236) and the 220-metre section along Kings Hall Road has no cycle lane. Elmer's End Road often has heavy traffic, so cautious riders may wish to walk the 200 metres into South Norwood Country Park.

Refreshments: Greenwich has an abundance of refreshment facilities. Ladywell Fields Park café is a convenient oasis along this sometimes isolated route. There is a superstore next to the blue bridge in Riverview Walk. Just behind Elmer's End station is a large superstore, and on Croydon Road there is a small parade of shops including a café and the William IV pub with outside seating.

This route starts by following the Ravensbourne River upstream from its confluence with the Thames at Deptford Creek, Greenwich, before joining a tributary, the Pool River in Catford. It continues along another tributary, Chaffinch Brook, all the way to the wild natural habitat of South Norwood Country Park. Here the open flat terrain creates a feeling of remoteness. The majority of the route follows Sustrans' NCN 21, known as the Waterlink Way.

BACKGROUND AND PLACES OF INTEREST
Waterways
The Ravensbourne River is 11 miles long, with a total catchment area of 112 miles. It flows into the Thames on the Tideway at Deptford, where its tidal reach is known as Deptford Creek. After Catford the route enters the Pool River flood plain, where there is a marked increase in trees and vegetation in contrast to the earlier urban industrial environment. There is an abundance of birdlife and smaller wildlife.

Ladywell Fields Park
The name 'Ladywell' is thought to have been derived from a well dedicated to the Virgin Mary. The site of the well is now under Ladywell railway station. Ladywell Fields was purchased in 1889 to serve the growing population of Lewisham and Catford. Prior to this the land was water meadows. In recent years, the park has had a makeover including removing the Ravensbourne from its former concrete channel and diverting it to form a new meandering river channel through the centre of the park, creating a wildlife area and natural habitat and building a café.

Starting Points & Transport:
1. Greenwich station – accessible via South Eastern services on the London Cannon Street to Slade Green Line. Also services from London Bridge, Charing Cross and Waterloo East stations. (Bikes are not allowed on the DLR.)
2. Greenwich Foot Tunnel.
3. Elmer's End Station: South Eastern services on Hayes to London Cannon Street Line. To return to Greenwich: four trains an hour, change at London Bridge, 40-50-minute journey.

Greenwich Council runs car parks in Cutty Sark Gardens, SE10, and also in Burney Street, SE10 – £1 per hour, no time limit. If driving, consider parking by Elmer's End Station and getting the train back to the start in Greenwich. (Pay and display parking is £4 for the day.)

Links to other routes
Route 08 – Tower Bridge to Greenwich.
Route 13 – The Isle of Dogs.

ROUTE INSTRUCTIONS:

1. Exit Greenwich Station.
   A) Confident riders can turn left onto Greenwich High Road (A 206) and continue into the one-way system. Take the right fork into Greenwich Church Street leading to the Cutty Sark and Greenwich Foot Tunnel on the Thames riverside.

Passing under the DLR viaduct in Broadway Fields Park.

   B) For a quieter but longer route, exit the station from Platform 1 using the wheelchair ramp to Tarves Way. Turn right onto the path that feeds into Straightmouth. At the fork in the road turn left along Randall Place. Turn right after the school onto Haddo Street. Pass around the diagonal barrier to stop cars and continue to the junction with Creek Road. Cross into Norway Street, turn right onto Thames Street, then take a left up Horseferry Place. Continue to the Thames riverside and turn right to reach the Cutty Sark clipper ship and the Greenwich Foot Tunnel entrance.

2. Cycle along the path away from the Cutty Sark, with the Thames on the right, and then join Horseferry Place. Look out for NCN 4 signs. Turn right into Thames Street; there is a restricted view of Deptford Creek through the gates at the end before the road leads into Norway Street. At the traffic lights, turn right onto Creek Road.

3. Over the bridge, leave the road at the toucan crossing.
   A) For a good view of Deptford Creek and where the Ravensbourne actually joins the Thames, take a brief diversion of less than 200 metres. Cross north over Creek Road at the toucan crossing and follow the NCN 4 signs.
   B) Otherwise, stay on the route and join Copperas Road, following NCN 21 signs. Turn left onto Creekside and the iridescent Laban Dance Centre. Turn left to take the pavement cycle lane down Deptford High Street (A2209) then turn left to a toucan crossing over Deptford Bridge (A2) and into Broadway Fields Park. Pass under the DLR viaduct and a Sustrans marker post. The first sighting of the Ravensbourne River is on the right, but when the path leads into Brookmills Park it starts to look more like a country river than a storm drain. Pass Elverson Road DLR station and then, after 180 metres, turn right through the car park and under the railway bridge.

4. Turn left onto Thurston Road, using the traffic island to get to the green pavement cycle lane. Take care crossing the entrance to the retail park and use the special cyclists' traffic light to cross over Loampit Vale (A2210). Turn left to cycle around Cornmill Gardens beside the viaduct and then along the river. Pass another distance marker and take the next right to Elmira Street and under the railway bridge. Turn left into quiet Marsala Road. At the end turn left onto Algernon Road, which filters to the left and up to the junction with busy Ladywell Road (B236).

5. Turn left and pass over the hump-backed railway bridge. Dismount to use the traffic island to cross and enter the park. Follow the route south next to the river and University Hospital Lewisham's new Riverside Wing. Next to Ladywell Athletic Arena, the route enjoyably utilises a spiral ramp to negotiate the railway line. The next 'lobe' of the park resembles a sports field rather than the manicured gardens of the first. After passing under the next railway line, the river is now on the left. At the bottom of the park, just short of Bourneville Road, pass left over a small bridge. Go under the railway line into a derelict area to join Adenmore Road.

6. Pass Catford Bridge station on the left and go under the Catford Road (A205) bridge to pick up the cycle path on the right. Carefully cross to the Halfords retail park but take the second entrance, leading to the second building. The railway line is on the right until the end of the road, where the route passes onto a tranquil river path again. Pass over the river and back over again near another Sustrans marker. From here the path widens. After the next crossing (near a playground) keep left, following the river on the wider path. The next section passes through the landscaped Riverview Walk and a park that was once an old gasworks. A blue tied-arch bridge marks the central point of the walk.

7. Cross Stanton Way (A2218) using the traffic island. Continue up Fambridge Close for 150 metres and join the path as the road bends away to the right. Pass another Sustrans marker before Lower Sydenham station, returning to the tarmac of Westerly Crescent.

8. Turn left onto Kangley Bridge Road, passing through a dreary industrial estate with an incongruous old village cricket green and pavilion towards the end of the road. Where

The iridescent Laban Dance Centre, surrounded by 'Tellytubby' lawns.

the road ends on the left, join the shared tarmac path with a white line down the middle. After 450 metres of densely wooded riverside path, emerge to cross Leonard Road and enter Cator Park. There is a Sustrans marker just inside the entrance, indicating 3 miles from Lewisham. The route through Cator Park is clearly defined by a white line separating cyclists from pedestrians. Turn right onto Kings Hall Road.

9. After 220 metres turn left into Station Approach, using the shared path to the right of the gravel road. Dismount to pass under Kent House station. Staying on unsealed roads, turn left at the crossroads onto Barnmead Road. Pass the grand Victorian houses of this affluent part of Beckenham and turn right, still on the same road.

10. At the crossroads with Beckenham Road (A234) turn left onto the green pavement cycle lane. It crosses a Total garage where the cycle lane gives way, so take care. Under the railway bridge (Beckenham Road station), use the toucan crossing and turn right into Churchfields Road. Keep following for 0.75 miles, all the way to the T-junction with busy Elmer's End Road. Turn left.

11. Cross at the toucan crossing and follow the narrow cycle lane left to enter the park. Pass through the trees and turn right onto the sandy path. After about 75 metres there is an option to walk down a footpath to a viewing platform over the large lake and wetland area. Cycle past another Sustrans

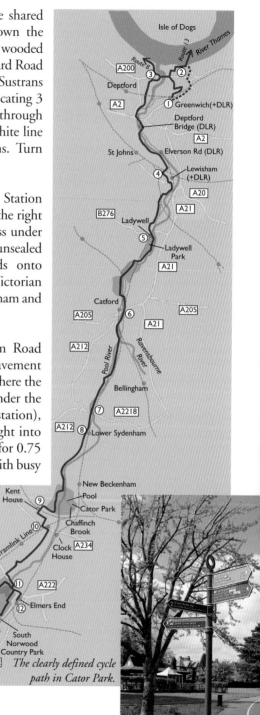

The clearly defined cycle path in Cator Park.

marker before the path bends to the left and opens out into the park. Straight ahead on the wider path is the visitors' centre with toilets and children's play area; further on, the track switches to cobbles leading up to the Tramlink line. Turn left and back onto the sandy track. Further on, it is worth diverting to the top of the mound for a good view of the park. The track goes downhill away from the tramline, along the side of some playing fields. Stay on the wider track, which winds its way back up to the lake and the entrance to Elmer's End Road.

12. Turn right and walk along the pavement, straight to Elmer's End station.

Distance: 8.85 miles – if terminated at Ponders End station. 17.8 miles – if including both detours and returning to Hackney Wick station. (The route can be shortened to 3.5 miles if terminated at Tottenham Hale.)

Map: OS Explorer map 173 and TfL Local Cycling Guides 2 and 4.

Surface and Gradients: Mainly flat river- and canal-side ride. Surfaces are all-weather gravel or sealed paths; a very short section of the route is on sealed roads. The towpath after Tottenham Lock deteriorates for a while.

Roads and road crossings: There is a half-mile section of Towpath Road (south of the North Circular Flyover) that HGV lorries have access to, so be alert. Also a section of the alternative route on Harbet Road is busy for about 500 metres, but this industrial area is much quieter at the weekend.

Refreshments: Nearby Victoria Park has a café, as does the WaterWorks Nature Reserve and Golf Centre just off Hackney Marshes. In Lea Bridge Road, a very short diversion off the route, there are the Princess of Wales and Ship Aground pubs. The Riverside Café is just north of Springfield Marina and there is a café and toilets in Springfield Park, adjacent to the marina on the west shore. There are many options in Tottenham Hale, only a few hundred metres from Tottenham Lock, and Stonebridge Lock has a café.

This is a linear route from Hackney Wick to Ponders End. It's a flat ride on good paths, so it's ideal to ride up and back, taking detours to Walthamstow Marshes and Banbury Reservoir. The route contains a string of marshes and reservoirs which bring the countryside into the urban sprawl of Greater London, on NCN 1.

BACKGROUND AND PLACES OF INTEREST

Waterworks

For much of London's history, private companies have supplied fresh water from the Rivers Thames and Lea. Waterworks were established at Lea Bridge before 1767, later acquired by the East London Waterworks Company (ELWC) which was founded by an Act of Parliament in 1806. The Metropolis Water Act of 1852 made it unlawful for any water company to extract water for domestic use from the tidal reaches of the Thames, and so forced the ELWC to look further up the Lee Valley for clean water. They purchased the Coppermill at Walthamstow and modified it to drive a water pump to assist in building reservoirs on nearby marshland. Most of London's water still comes from the Rivers Thames and Lea.

Lee Valley Park

In Saxon times the River Lea formed a natural boundary between the kingdoms of Essex and Middlesex. In the 1770s the digging of Hackney Cut brought about a change in the landscape. It was further altered when rubble from the air raids of World War 2 was dumped there. More recently, two nature reserves have been founded to the north of Hackney Marshes: the Waterworks Nature Reserve houses one of London's biggest bird hides and the Middlesex Filterbeds Nature Reserve is a 4-hectare oasis of open water, reed bed and mature woodland. Walthamstow Marshes has been designated a Site of Special Scientific Interest (SSSI) and Tottenham Marshes is carefully managed to encourage the public to enjoy the open space and protect its wildlife. The southern end of the Lee Valley is currently being developed as part of the 2012 Olympics site.

Starting Points & Transport:

1. Hackney Wick station – accessible via London Overground train services on the North London Line running between Richmond and Stratford.
2. Hackney Marshes car park.
3. Tottenham Hale station: National Express East Anglia train services on Tottenham Vale branch of the Lea Valley line from London Liverpool Street.
4. Ponders End station: National Express East Anglia train services on Tottenham Vale branch of the Lea Valley line from London Liverpool Street.

There is free parking on the streets in the areas north of Victoria Park and Hackney Wick station. There is also the option to park in Hackney Marshes car park on the Homerton Road (B112) and join the route at (4).

Links to other routes
Route 10 – Limehouse Basin and Limehouse Cut Loop.
Route 11 – Grand Union Canal Regent's Branch.
Route 25 – Epping Forest (2.3 miles to the east).

ROUTE INSTRUCTIONS:

1. Exit Hackney Wick station from Platform 2 (trains from Stratford) onto Wallis Road. Turn left and go under the railway bridge, turning left again onto Hepscott Road. This is where the exit from Platform 1 (trains from Richmond) emerges. Keep going straight ahead for 100 metres. Turn left onto Rothbury Road, which becomes White Post Lane and leads to a bridge over the River Lea Navigation.

2. Go down the ramp and double back under the bridge beside the Hackney Cut. The route now follows NCN 1, so look out for signs on wooden posts. The Olympic Park is on the right. Pass under the North London Line railway bridge. After 600 metres, pass under the small road bridge (Eastway, A106) and large double flyover (East Cross Route, A12).

3. After one more bridge (Homerton Road, B112) the route passes Hackney Marshes on the right, which boasts the highest concentration of football pitches in Europe. After passing the footbridge over the canal, the route leaves the Hackney Cut and heads to the right-hand edge of the pitches.

4. Cross the distinctive red Friends Bridge and pass to the right of the Waterworks Nature Reserve. Pass a Sustrans 3-kilometre marker. To visit the café and toilets turn right, cross the nature reserve and go over the footbridge leading to the WaterWork Nature Reserve and Golf Centre (approximately 350 metres). Pass under the Lea Bridge Road (A104) and enter the section through Walthamstow Marshes. From here the route splits, giving two ways around the marshes:

Barges near Springfield Marina.

A) Climb up from under the Lea Bridge Road, stay on the path following a levee across the marshes and pass Lee Valley Regional Park Riding Centre on the right. After a further 500 metres keep right and dip down under the two railway lines. The path bends left and crosses Coppermill Stream before joining Coppermill Lane. Turn left under the very low railway crossing (5 feet!) and follow the road around to Springfield Marina. This section is approximately 1.1 miles.

B) Climb up from under the Lea Bridge Road and take the first left to go across the open field behind Lee Valley Ice Centre. Turn right on the towpath, heading north. (Or turn left to visit the Princess of Wales or Ship Aground pubs.) Pass under the railway bridge. Walthamstow Marshes Nature Reserve is on the right. Look under the arches for the blue plaque commemorating the first all-British powered flight from the marshes in 1909. After 500 metres follow the path around the bend next to the marina. Turn left onto the roadway to rejoin the main route. This section is approximately 1 mile.

5. Walk over the bridge across the River Lea Navigation. Turn left to enter Springfield Park. Turn right past the Riverside Café to continue north, with West Warwick Reservoir across the canal to the east. After 0.6 miles pass under a railway bridge, with another one following 500 metres later.

6. Pass under Ferry Lane (A503) to reach Tottenham Lock (NCN 1 diverts to the left of this route). Move up to road level and follow the cycle lane to Tottenham Hale station if you wish to end the ride early. Carry on between the canal on the left and the river on the right. The path deteriorates a little from here as it passes between Tottenham Marshes and Lockwood Reservoir.

7. After another 0.6 miles, you arrive at Stonebridge Lock. From here the route splits, giving two ways to reach the passage under the North Circular Road (A406):
A) Cross over the lock, joining up with NCN 1 again. After 500 metres turn right and cross the bridge and then the open ground.*** Cross another bridge and take the road towards the houses. Turn left before Sandpiper Close, keeping the Banbury Reservoir on the left, leading onto Folly Lane and up to a roundabout. Turn left onto Harbet Road and continue up to the roundabout. Take the first exit and turn off the road onto the red cycle lane, turning right to pass under the huge North Circular flyover. This option is 2 miles long.

B) Continue on the west side of the canal for just over half a mile, passing through Lee Valley Regional Park. Cross over the bridge to continue northwards on the opposite bank, rejoining NCN 1. This section plunges into an industrial landscape for a short while. Join a wide cement track that changes to a rough tarmac road and carry on to Towpath Road. Beware of the HGV lorries turning in this area. Pass under the North Circular flyover. This option is more direct and is 1.25 miles long.

8. Stay on the towpath and pass under a small road bridge (Lee Park Way). 0.8 miles ahead is the next landmark, Pickett's Lock. (Built in 1770. Hopefully there will be no reason to notice the sewage works across the canal.) The high grassy bank on the right hides the William Girling Reservoir.

9. Keep heading north for 1 mile to where the canal splits and there is a car park on the right. Have a look at Ponders End Lock before returning to take the ramp up to street level onto Wharf Road, turning left to get to Ponders End station. At the hairpin bend leave the road and take the ramp up and over Meridian Way (A1055), toward the station.

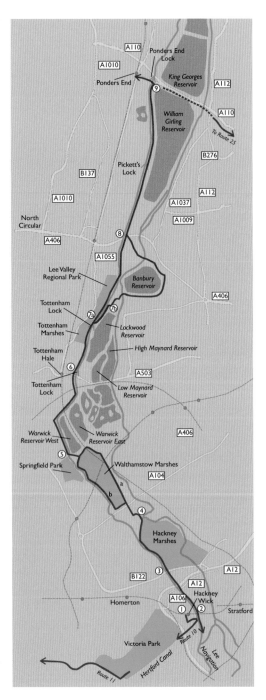

Distance: 7.2 miles in Richmond Park. Add 2.35 miles if starting and finishing from Richmond station.

Map: Ordnance Survey Explorer map 161 and TfL Local Cycling Guides 9/10.

Surface and Gradients: Gently undulating, but with a few short sharp climbs. The route is the off-road golden gravel track called the Tamsin Trail, but there is also a choice of tarmac roads which criss-cross the park should you wish to lengthen it.

Roads and road crossings: Short sections of the routes are busy at times. Inside the park are six road crossings; take care, as most of these junctions are at the gates where traffic can build up. No commercial vehicles are allowed into the park, and a blanket 20mph speed limit means that even the tarmac road is a joy to cycle on.

Refreshments: At Pembroke Lodge, there is a snack bar. There is also the grander buffet-style Pembroke Lodge and Gardens Café within the house (although sweaty bikers may feel conspicuous). Roehampton Gate Café sells a range of snacks, drinks and ice creams with indoor and outdoor seating. In the summer, Broomfield Hill and Robin Hood Gate are two refreshment points selling a wide range of hot and cold snacks and beverages.

Richmond Park is a rare and beautiful area of open countryside situated in the suburbs of Southwest London. Charles I founded the park in 1625 for hunting red and fallow deer. He is said to have bought it to escape the plague in London. Today, modern Londoners go there to escape the noisy claustrophobia of a capital city. The ride principally follows the Tasmin trail, a good all-weather family cycle route which is very safe as well as interesting.

BACKGROUND AND PLACES OF INTEREST

Pembroke Lodge

It is hard to believe this magnificent Georgian Mansion started out as a mole catcher's one-room cottage *c.*1750. It was known as Hill Lodge when George III granted it to his 'close friend' the Countess of Pembroke in 1787. Over the next 9 years she extended the building. After being passed on to the Prime Minister, Lord John Russell, in 1847, many illustrious visitors were entertained there, including Queen Victoria, Garibaldi and writers such as Dickens, Tennyson and Thackeray. Between 1876 and 1894 it was home to Bertrand Russell. During World War 2 it housed the GHQ Liaison Regiment. It is now privately owned and run as a hotel. The gardens and café are open to the public.

White Lodge

Now the country home of the Royal Ballet School, this Palladian villa was commissioned by George II for use as a hunting lodge in 1727 and has been the home to many royals since. In 1861 Queen Victoria and Prince Albert came to White Lodge to mourn her recently departed mother. In 1894 Edward VIII was born at the lodge. The Duke and Duchess of York (later George VI and Queen Elizabeth) lived here for a few years after their marriage in 1923. The Sadler's Wells Ballet School was granted the use of the lodge on a permanent basis in 1955. In recent years it has relocated its ballet museum to White Lodge. It is open to the public but advanced booking is required.

King Henry's Mound

Well worth the short walk from the Tamsin Trail to enjoy the panoramic view. Created in 1710, it gives a clear view all the way to St Paul's Cathedral, 15 miles away.

Wildlife

Although Richmond Park is famous for its deer, it also has a wide variety of other wildlife such as birds, squirrels and rabbits. On an even smaller scale, it is a Special Area of Conservation for its population of stag beetles. There are approximately 63 species of birds breeding here. You may wish to take a diversion to the Pen Ponds between Ham Gate and Robin Hood Gate to see the waterfowl.

Starting Points and Parking:

1. Pembroke Lodge car park, situated between Richmond and Ham Gate.
2. Richmond station – accessible via frequent services on South West Trains' Reading-Waterloo line. The North London Line runs from Richmond to Stratford and opens up the vast London overground network via Willesden Junction. Richmond is also on a loop including Twickenham, Kingston, Wimbledon and Clapham Junction.
3. Norbiton station – accessible via frequent services on the Shepperton-Waterloo line.

There are six car parks within Richmond Park. This is a circular ride so it can be started from any park gate along the perimeter.

Links to other routes

Route 01 – Kingston to Teddington Lock via Hampton Court Palace. (via Ham Gate Avenue).
Route 02 – Ham Common to Richmond Lock Loop (via Ham Gate Avenue).
Route 19 – Wimbledon Common and Putney Heath (via Robin Hood Gate).

ROUTE INSTRUCTIONS:

1. A: From Richmond station: exit and turn right. Walk the short distance to Church Road, which is a 'no right turn' junction. Proceed up Church Road and cross over the A305, taking the first right into Dynevor Road. Turn left up Mount Ararat Road. Take the third right into Chislehurst Road and turn left up Onslow Road. Continue straight into Marlborough Road. Turn right onto busy Queens Road (with a zebra crossing on the left if needed). Turn immediately left into Cambrian Road. Join the park through the

The road passing through Richmond Park.

kissing gate at the end. Walk the short distance to the Tamsin Trail and turn left.
B: From Norbiton station: go straight down Wolverton Avenue, to the right of the station entrance. At the T-junction turn right onto Kingston Hill (A308), then immediately left into Queens Road. This junction can be busy so use the pedestrian crossing. Queens Road leads to Kingston Gate. Enter the park and turn left off the road onto the Tamsin Trail, where there are green markings. Go to stage 4.
C: From Pembroke Lodge Car Park pick up the Tasmin Trail, a hard-packed sandy path running between the car park and the café. Follow it due north (left on leaving the toilet/café buildings) slightly uphill to Richmond Gate. Look out for the path to King Henry's Mound on the left, after the thatched building. Carefully cross the Sawyer's Hill road at Richmond Gate. The route from Richmond station joins about 440 metres further on.

2. Proceed clockwise around the park following the sandy path and signs. Take care crossing the tarmac roads. The next road crossing is the Sheen Gate. Pass Adams Pond on the right. Just before the Roehampton Gate, take care crossing the wooden bridge in wet weather. Head south through the wooded section of the trail, emerging at the Robin Hood Gate.

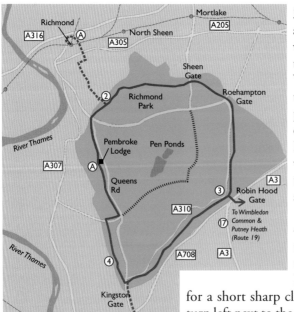

3. The trail gradually ascends along this section with some steep climbs towards Broomfield Hill Wood. The trail then drops to cross the Ladderstile Gate path, which is pedestrian only. Continue to the busy Kingston Gate, taking care when crossing. This is where the route from Norbiton station joins.

4. Follow the gradual fall of the Tamsin Trail before turning right to cross the Ham Gate road. Turn right for a short sharp climb up the hill. At the top turn left next to the tarmac crossroad, where the trail gradually climbs back to the Pembroke Lodge car park.

Distance: 7 miles from Southside Common (3). Add an extra 0.85 miles if starting from Wimbledon station (1).

Map: OS Explorer map 161 and TfL Local Cycling Guides 9 or 10.

Surfaces and Gradients: Some steep sections up from the Robin Hood Ride entrance (from the Robin Hood Roundabout, A3). These are also the roughest. Most other paths are well-drained gravel paths. A mountain bike with knobbly tyres would be best unless ridden after a long spell of dry weather. The steep hill up from Wimbledon Station will tire all but the fittest riders.

Roads and road crossings: The route is busy near Wimbledon station, so walk around the corner into St Georges Road. Worple Road can also be busy but the short section is easily walked. Cannizaro Road (B281), which bisects part of the common, is busy but easily crossed. The subways under Tibbet's Corner make crossing the A3 onto Putney Heath perfectly safe. On Wimbledon Common the route is safe for children, but they may need some bike-handling skills on the off-road Robin Hood ride.

Refreshments: The Fox and Grapes pub is on Camp Road. Wimbledon Windmill has an old-fashioned tearoom serving fry-ups as well as cakes and teas. There are two good pubs in Woodhayes Road, just south of the common – The Hand in Hand and The Crooked Billet, both opposite a picturesque village green. The Telegraph pub, a snack kiosk and toilets are on Putney Heath.

Wimbledon Common and adjoining Putney Heath are a welcome oasis of wild common land in Southwest London. This route can be considered child friendly if starting the ride from Southside Common, but parents may choose to walk their children along Portsmouth Road (on the Putney Heath section).

BACKGROUND AND PLACES OF INTEREST

Putney Heath

Part of Wimbledon and Putney Commons, this was a notorious place for duels and highwaymen in the 18th century. Tibbet's Corner was once the site of a gallows, now it's a roundabout. The heath consists of woods and grassland and a number of ponds, while Wimbledon and Putney Commons overall contain the largest heathland habitat in the London area. Much of the Commons is a Site of Special Scientific Interest and a Special Area of Conservation.

Wimbledon Common

The windmill has been a distinctive landmark on the common since 1817, but it was only used as a working mill until the late 1800s. Robert Baden-Powell wrote Scouting for Boys in the Mill House in 1908. The mill itself has since been restored and contains a museum of milling.

Cannizaro Park (off Westside Common)

The 34 acres of gardens are situated in the grounds of Cannizaro House, a Grade II Georgian mansion which adopted its name in 1832, when the leaseholder succeeded to the Sicilian dukedom of Cannizzaro. In the 1980s it became a hotel, but the gardens are the property of the council and are open to the public.

Starting Points & Transport:

1. Wimbledon Station (1) – accessible via South West Trains' mainline services from Waterloo, and First Capital Connect/Southern services on the Sutton loop.
2. Southside Common (3).

The Windmill Museum on the common has a large free car park. There is also a smaller free car park at the top of Sunset Road (off Camp Road) and free parking on parts of Westside. Parking is also possible on the estate off Putney Heath, as far as Dover Park Drive.

Links to other routes

Putney Bridge, just down the hill from the common, is a connection/nodal point to both Route 05 and Route 06. Route 18 – Richmond Park is just over the busy Kingston Bypass (A3), but it has a cycle route with a bike-friendly Pegasus crossing.

ROUTE INSTRUCTIONS:

1. Exit Wimbledon station and use the pedestrian crossing to walk across Wimbledon Bridge Road (A219), turning right. Turn left onto St George's Road. Start cycling. After 170 metres the road bends right but proceed straight ahead, down the green cycle lane and onto the quiet residential street.

2. At the T-junction turn right up Tabor Grove. Turn left onto Worple Road and then immediate right, up Ridgeway Place (cautious cyclists may walk the 40 metres to Ridgeway Place). Go straight at the crossroads into The Grange and continue onto the T-junction with Southside Common.

3. Go straight onto the sandy path to the right of Rushmere Pond. Join the larger path and veer to cross Cannizaro Road. Continue straight until you join a crossroads. Carefully turn right onto the sandy track that runs parallel to West Place.

4. After the road bends to the left, the path forks. Take the right-hand fork and enter the trees. Cross a gallop after 150 metres (look out for horses) and keep going straight ahead for 380 metres before crossing another horse trail. Continue straight, joining a wide dirt road (Windmill Road) and heading towards the Windmill.

5. Rejoin the sealed road (beware of cars from the Windmill Museum car park). Leave the road, passing around a green metal gate. After 150 metres the path forks again through some trees. Take the right-hand fork. Go straight over a crossroads path (used by horses and bikes). After 650 metres the path emerges onto a grassy area; keeping to the left-hand path. Enter the underpass for Tibbet's Corner roundabout, keeping on the right-hand side (the left is for horses).

6. Emerge up onto road level at Tibbet's Ride. Turn sharp left along a cycle path, keeping the hedge to your right. Follow it around through a car park and past the Telegraph pub. You are now on Putney Heath.

Wimbledon Common Windmill.

7. At the cross-roads with Wildcroft Road there is the option to turn right to reach the toilets and café kiosk, 600 metres past the mini-roundabout.

8. To remain en route, cross over the junction and take the first left into Portsmouth Road. When the road ends, continue on the path through the dense woods. The path bends to the left, passing Scio Pond and under the Kingston Road (A3). Keep to the right-hand fork in the path where the trees are less dense. Eventually the path rejoins that taken earlier and crosses the road to the Windmill.

9. Continue back-tracking but keep going south (don't take the earlier path to the left). Pass the golf course, enter the trees and look out for horses on the gallop.

10. Windmill Road ends at a small triangle of grass. Turn right along Robin Hood Road. At the car park the road stops and the dirt path (Robin Hood Ride) starts. This section can get muddy after rainfall. The path falls about 40 metres over ¾ of a mile.

11. At the bottom, near a bridge and a white wooden gate, the route turns right. (Be careful not to turn too sharply, onto Lower Gravelly Ride horse path.) The route under the trees following Beverley Brook is undulating and enjoyable. The boundary of the common is reached where the path emerges next to playing fields. To carry on to Richmond Park, pass over the bridge with a post bearing a Capital Ring badge.

12. Turn around and retrace the route back uphill to the small grass triangle where Windmill Road and Robin Hood Road conjoin.

13. Carry on past the junction through a gate onto Camp Road, which passes Wimbledon Golf Club on the right and the Fox and Grapes pub on the left. At the crossroads, return to the off-road path ahead (from the start of the route) and continue back to Rushmere Pond.

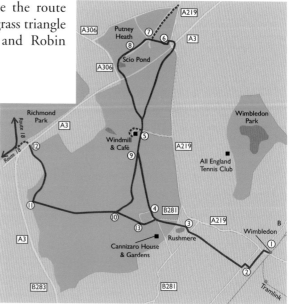

Distance: The central route is 7.2 miles. Add 2.3 miles if starting from Waterloo station. Add 1.3 miles if starting from Paddington station.

Map: Ordnance Survey Explorer map 173 and TfL Local Cycling Guides 1 or 7.

Surfaces and Gradients: This is a flat ride. Surfaces are sealed roads and paths.

Roads and road crossings: Once within the parks, the route is on quiet roads or paths. Coming from Waterloo station, Westminster Bridge Road (A302) is busy but has a crossing point and bus lane. Parliament Square is also busy and is best walked across, enabling you to savour views of the Houses of Parliament. If the section from Birdcage Walk to Buckingham Palace is too busy, it is also enjoyable to dismount and walk across the bottom of St James Park, joining up with the route again over The Mall. Going to and from Paddington station, the short sections of Praed Street and London Street are busy but can be walked.

Refreshments: Within Hyde Park there are many kiosks, as well as the Serpentine Bar & Kitchen restaurant with outside seating area. Green Park has a refreshment point and toilet next to Canada Gate.

Become a tourist in the heart of London on a route that passes many famous landmarks: the London Eye, Big Ben, the Houses of Parliament and Buckingham Palace to name but a few. The three Royal Parks offer a refuge from the often chaotic traffic, and it is no wonder they are often referred to as 'the lungs of London'. Children could cycle the part of the route within Hyde Park.

BACKGROUND AND PLACES OF INTEREST
The London Eye
Since opening in March 2000 the London Eye has become an iconic landmark, drawing over 3.5 million visitors each year. It is a breathtaking feat of design and engineering by husband and wife team David Marks and Julia Barfield. The wheel design

The London Eye.

was intended as a metaphor for the end of the 20th century and time moving on into the new millennium. Being 443 feet high and weighing 2100 tonnes, it was a major task just to winch it up vertically, in October 1999, to its position over the Thames. Each of its 32 capsules offers a completely new perspective of London for up to 25 miles in all directions. With an almost imperceptible speed of 26 centimetres per second, each 'flight' or rotation takes 30 minutes.

Wellington Arch
George IV planned both the Wellington Arch and Marble Arch as commemorations of victory in the Napoleonic Wars. The neoclassical Wellington Arch, designed by Decimus Burton, was erected in 1830 as a ceremonial entrance to Buckingham Palace. In 1846 the arch was topped by a massive statue, by Matthew Cotes, of the First Duke of Wellington (Sir Arthur Wellesley) riding a horse. 36 years later the monument was moved to Hyde Park Corner, and in 1912 the Wellesley statue was replaced by an angel of peace in a quadriga (a chariot drawn by four horses abreast). Created by Adrian Jones, it is said to be the largest bronze statue in Europe. In the 1960s traffic was routed around the arch, leaving it somewhat stranded. From the 1950s up until 1992, it served as London's second smallest police station (the smallest is in Trafalgar Square). Since English Heritage took over the structure in

1999, visitors can take a lift up to the balconies just below the statue for fantastic views across the surrounding area. The Wellington Arch is now also known as Constitution Arch due to its location on Constitution Hill.

Starting Points & Transport:
1. Waterloo Station – via South West Trains services south and west of London.
2. Paddington Station – via Great Western services on the Greenford branch line and to the west of London.
3. The car park south of the Serpentine Bridge, London W2.
There are multi-storey car parks around the South Bank charging £14 per day (half price on Sundays and Bank Holidays). Some parking is possible around Waterloo on Sundays. In Hyde Park there is pay and display parking (maximum stay of 2 hours) along West Carriage Drive. The route lies within the Congestion Charge Zone.

Links to other routes
Route 07 – Waterloo to Tower Bridge.
Route 11 – Grand Union Canal: Regent's Branch.
Route 12 – Grand Union Canal: Paddington Branch to Brentford Lock

ROUTE INSTRUCTIONS:
1. A) Leave Waterloo station via the exit opposite Platforms 12 and 13. On the opposite side of the road, slightly to the left, there is a green cycle lane marked by a high granite kerb. Be polite and give pedestrians and tourists right of way. Follow the cycle lane downhill, over York Road (A3200) and under the railway bridge. Dismount on reaching the road. Turn left, walking along Concert Hall Approach (one way) for only 65 metres until turning left onto Belvedere Road to cycle past a wonderful view of the London Eye and County Hall on the right.
B) Exit Paddington station, turn left and walk across London Street. Use the traffic lights to cross the incredibly busy Praed Street and continue straight ahead until the mini-roundabout. Turn immediate left again into Gloucester Square. Continue straight up to the T-junction and turn right onto Hyde Park Crescent. Follow around into Tichborne Row. Continue over the crossroads into Albion Street. Cycle-friendly traffic lights lead into the park through the Albion Gate. Go to (8).
C) Exit the Serpentine car park and turn right; go to (7).

2. Pass through the narrow gap of the traffic barrier up to Westminster Bridge Road. Turn right using the crossing and join the bus lane to cross the bridge. Confident riders can negotiate around Parliament Square to turn left down Great George Street. Otherwise dismount and walk, using the pedestrian crossings.

Looking across the Serpentine at the Lido.

3. Carry on down Birdcage Walk, passing St James Park on the right and the Guards Museum on the left. At the traffic lights turn right, passing Buckingham Palace and the Victoria Memorial, before entering onto Constitutional Hill. Dismount and use the pedestrian crossing to enter Green Park (next to Canada Gate).

4. Turn left to pick up the cycle path adjacent to the sandy horse gallops. At the end take the toucan over the five lanes of Duke of Wellington Place (A4). Pass around the arch and up towards the right to take the toucan crossings and cycle lanes into Hyde Park. Go straight ahead over Carriage Drive and left onto the cycle lane adjacent to Rotten Row. This continues for up to a mile with good views of the Serpentine on the right. Pass the Princess of Wales Memorial Fountain towards the end of this section, on the right.

5. Use the pedestrian crossing, join the cycle path opposite and turn left towards Alexandra Gate. After 150 metres the cycle lane ends at the ornate Coalbrookdale Gate. Pass through the gates onto Albert Approach Road. The Albert Memorial is just ahead on the right. Now retrace your route to the last pedestrian crossing but turn left into the park at Mount Gate.

6. Take the only cycle path straight ahead, past Round Pond up to the Broad Walk. From here Kensington Palace can be visited on foot. Return the same way to exit at Mount Gate. Turn left onto the cycle path.

7. Pass the car park and continue over the Serpentine Bridge, after which the road bends right and then left. Turn right after the bend, using the pedestrian island to cross over the road, across the sandy gallops (North Ride) and left onto the shared path. Follow the path to the top of the park near Victoria Gate and turn right to join the cycle lane on North Carriage Drive.

8. Pass Albion Gate. (Note: the return journey from Albion Gate to Paddington station is a little different due to the one-way system. Once on Hyde Park Crescent, continue ahead as it becomes Southwick Street. Turn left into Star Street, right into Norfolk Place and finally left onto Praed Street.)

9. After 25 metres turn right to the tree-lined Broad Walk (with a cycle refuge in the middle of the road). Follow for 1 kilometre all the way down to Queen Elizabeth Gate. Turn right for the Serpentine Bar & Kitchen restaurant or carry on to enjoy views of the Serpentine, and maybe an ice cream.

10. Go back down Serpentine Road, turn right and retrace the route past Wellington Arch and along Green Park to Canada Gate. Carry on along the path adjacent to The Mall. Pass the Duke of York Column on your left and turn right into Horse Guards Road. Pass Horse Guards Parade on the left. Keep an eye out for the pelicans that inhabit Duck Island to the right of St James Park.

11. At the T-junction, turn left into Great George Street to retrace the route back to Waterloo or right into Birdcage Walk if you started from Paddington or the Serpentine car park. Go to (3).

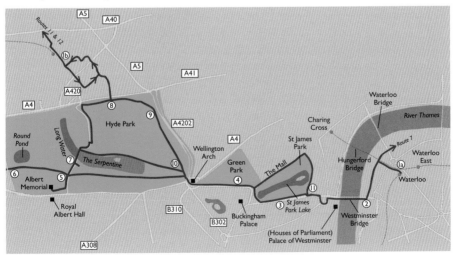

Distance: 12 miles.

Map: OS Explorer map 173 and TfL Local Cycling Guides 14, or 4 and 7.

Surfaces and Gradients: Generally a flat ride but there are gruelling hills heading up to and around Hampstead Heath. The route is on tarmac roads except for on the heath itself, where the surfaces are mostly sandy gravel and some sealed paths.

Roads and road crossings: Although minor roads are followed, some are very busy. Care is needed on the short section of Hampstead Road (A400) near Euston station (1). There is a 240-metre stretch on College Crescent (6) which is busy, while the road at Swiss Cottage is also narrow. Take care crossing Arkwright Road, Finchley (7). North End Way is a steep twisty section of road with no pavement but with a footpath for the more prudent cyclist (8). East Heath Road and South End Road can also be busy (10).

Refreshments: Regent's Park has several refreshment sites. Within the Inner Circle is the Garden Café; along the Broad Walk there are the Cow and Bean Café and the Honest Sausage. There is also a grand old four-spouted water tap a short walk up Hanover Gate (to the left of the Boathouse Café). Surrounding Hampstead Heath are many pubs, notably The Bull and Bush (North Road) and The Spaniards Inn (Spaniards Road, following the cycle lane).

This is a linear route starting with a gentle warm-up around Regents Park before a climb up to Hampstead Heath. Between the two parks are many blue plaques which celebrate great figures of London's past.

BACKGROUND AND PLACES OF INTEREST

Regent's Park

One of the Royal Parks, with an area of 410 acres, Regent's Park has the largest grass area for sports in Central London. Once one of Henry VIII's hunting parks, it is mainly open parkland, with a lake, an open-air theatre, the London Zoo and numerous cafés and restaurants. The park has an outer ring road called the Outer Circle (2.7 miles long) and an inner ring road called the Inner Circle. The most carefully tended section, Queen Mary's Gardens, is located within the Inner Circle.

Hampstead Heath

A few miles north of Central London, Hampstead Heath feels like the heart of the English countryside. It is located on a sandy ridge and is one of the highest points in London. The landscape is varied and includes woodland, meadows and heath land. There are over 25 ponds located in clusters along the valleys.

Starting Points and Parking:

1. Euston station – accessible via London Overground services along the Watford line.
2. London Zoo car park (3).
3. Hampstead station – accessible via London Overground services. Change at Willesden Junction for Euston.

The zoo car park is £12.50 per day (Sundays and public holidays £1.20/hr, no limit). There is also pay-and-display on the Outer Circle at Regent's Park.

Hampstead Heath's 'mixed pond' on the right and pond no. 2 on the left.

Links to other routes

Route 11 – Grand Union Canal: Regent's Branch.
Route 22 – The Parkland Walk and Finsbury Park (1.25 miles east).

ROUTE INSTRUCTIONS:

1. Exit Euston station following the signs for the Transport Police, turning right out of the mainline platforms onto Melton Street and then right again into Cardington Street. Turn left at the T-junction onto Hampstead Road (A400) and first right onto Robert Street. Continue all the way to the end. At the traffic lights continue

straight into Chester Close South. Follow around to the left. Pass through the arch and take the right turn onto Chester Gate. Turn right onto the Outer Circle.

2. Turn left onto Chester Road. At the zebra crossing turn right on to Broad Walk, or if it's closed stay on the Outer Circle to (3).

3. Emerge from the park, turn left back onto the Outer Circle and pass the zoo. Keep going around the park, passing Central London Mosque on the right and the traffic lights at Hanover Gate. Continue until the major crossroads and traffic lights on the south side of the park. Turn left onto York Bridge and left again into the Inner Circle to pass the Garden Café.

4. Turn left into Chester Road and left again onto the Outer Circle, re-passing the zoo again. Turn right onto Avenue Road just after the running track. The climb up to Hampstead starts here. Carry straight on for 800 metres then turn right onto the quieter Elsworthy Road. There is a pedestrian crossing here if the road is busy. Turn left into Wadham Gardens and left again onto Harley Road.

5. Take the cycle lane in the middle of the road and go straight on at the traffic lights into Winchester Road. Turn left onto Eton Road and cross the shared pedestrian area.

6. Wheel your bike right and use the pedestrian crossing to pass Northways Parade and proceed up College Crescent. The gradients increase from here. After 240 metres turn left, opposite Freud's statue, onto Maresfield Gardens. Pass Freud's house just before turning left into Nutley Terrace, then turn right onto Neterhall Gardens. Turn left down Neterhall Way to cut through to Frognal.

7. Turn right here to start a long steep climb up to the crossing of busy Arkwright Road. Frognal bends to the left just before the top of the hill and becomes Frognal Rise before running into Branch Hill. Drop downhill to the junction with West Heath Road which is on a bend. Continue downhill on West Heath Road for 500 metres. Turn off right onto the Sandy Road path opposite Platt's Lane. As it is on a bend, take care turning right.

The route passes London Zoo,
where giraffes can often be seen.

8. Pass the gate to Golders Hill Park on the left and join the tarmac section of Sandy Road to the T-junction with North End Way opposite the Old Bull and Bush pub. Cautious riders should dismount and take the footpath to the right up the steep hill. More confident riders can turn right and climb up the unpaved North End Way for 300 metres to where the footpath rejoins the road. Pass Jack Straw's Castle pub on the mini-roundabout and turn left onto Spaniards Road.

9. After 80 metres turn right onto the sandy shared path which runs downhill. Cycle-friendly paths are marked by a yellow cyclist symbol on the ground. Note there is a 12-mph speed limit on the heath, not to mention lots of dogs and children running around. Take the right fork and pass downhill between the mixed bathing pond on the right and No. 2 pond on the left. Continue to the large car park and water fountain.

10. Turn left to join East Heath Road, which becomes South End Road. Take the first left onto Parliament Hill, cycling uphill past Hampstead Heath station and keeping right. At the top, turn right into Nassington Road and drop down to enter the heath again. There are far more pedestrians (especially children) at the weekend, so ride with consideration.

11. Turn left on to Highgate Road and carry on past the mini-roundabout to Highgate West Hill. Go straight uphill to turn left into Millfield Lane. Follow around and up the hill to the entrance to Hampstead Heath, on your left. Pass between Highgate Men's Bathing Pond on the left and Model Boating Pond on the right. Continue uphill to join the path again that runs down past No. 2 pond. Follow the same route towards the car park and to Hampstead Heath station.

Distance: 6.2 miles – if starting and finishing at Finsbury Park station. 5.7 miles – if starting and finishing at Holmesdale Road.

Map: OS Explorer map 173 and TfL Local Cycling Guides 4 or 14.

Surfaces and Gradients: Along Parkland Walk there is a gentle incline. The surface is well-drained hard-packed gravel. Finsbury Park is situated on a slight hill. All surfaces are sealed.

Roads and road crossings: Within Finsbury Park there is a circular tarmac road around its perimeter, which is closed to traffic apart from the quarter which runs from the top of the park past the Hornsey Gate entrance. This section is basically a car park and younger riders may be better off walking it.

Refreshments: Finsbury Park has a café, toilets and a water tap by the entrance to the staff yard.

This route is an almost totally traffic-free ride and safe to take children on. The return downhill to Finsbury Park is a fine reward for little legs. The start follows a disused railway line along an embankment, giving views into back gardens or onto busy roads from the bridges. Towards the opposite end the route runs along a densely wooded cutting. There is lively and creative graffiti on most brick surfaces along the Parkland Walk and there have been very occasional muggings of lone bikers after dark. This pleasant circuit leads finally to the café and boating pond. It is advisable to check the internet for when big events are held in Finsbury Park or when Arsenal have a home game, as this can make parking or even cycling to the park quite difficult. The more ambitious rider may wish to push on for 1.25 miles from the Holmesdale Road end of the route through hilly but picturesque Highgate to take Route 21 in reverse, or join Route 17 less than 1.85 miles to the west.

BACKGROUND AND PLACES OF INTEREST:
The Parkland Walk
The Parkland Walk follows the track bed of the disused London and North Eastern Railway line that ran between Finsbury Park and Alexandra Palace. It is London's longest local nature reserve. Trees and vegetation along a railway line are normally pruned back but for over 40 years the trees have been able to flourish, creating a linear woodland of many tree varieties. Wildlife has also thrived including a rare species of deer (muntjac), wildflowers and butterflies.

Finsbury Park
Stretching over 46 hectares, it gives inner London a wonderful green space that includes a mix of open ground, formal gardens, avenues of mature trees and an arboretum area. The Grade II listed park was officially opened in 1869, but its origins as a green space stretch further back. In the 15th century the area was a large woodland estate used for hunting, known as Brownswood. In 1750 a large manor house in the estate changed its name to Hornsey Wood House and became a popular

A couple of families enjoy the safe environment of the Parkland Walk.

The road leading back uphill to the café in Finsbury Park.

teahouse with 'pleasure grounds'. By 1796 the woodland had shrunk and the lake as it is known today was built. In 1986, after the demise of the GLC, the local council could not afford to maintain the park and it slipped into decline. Between 1996 and 2002, Heritage/Lottery funding returned many of the park's original features to their former glory. This included the re-landscaping of the American Gardens and Alexander McKenzie's historical flower gardens.

Starting Points & Transport:
1. Finsbury Park station – accessible via First Capital Connect Services to Kings Cross and Moorgate via Welwyn Garden City and Hertford North. Parking within Finsbury Park (2) or Holmesdale Road (6), entrance off Archway Road.
2. Crouch Hill Station (4) entails a 450-metre ride up quiet Crouch Hill Road – the station is accessible via the London overground service on the Barking-Gospel Oak Line.

There is parking at Finsbury Park via the Hornsey Gate entrance (Endymion Rd, N4). There is no parking when a major event is taking place. There is some parking on the streets around the Holmesdale Road entrance, e.g. at Shepherds Hill Heights.

Links to other routes
Route 17 – The River Lea Navigation (1.85 miles east).
Route 21 – Regent's Park to Hampstead Heath (1.25 miles west).

ROUTE INSTRUCTIONS:
1. Exit Finsbury Park station and turn left up Station Place. Turn left onto Stroud Green Road and immediately right, around the side of Rowans Tenpin Bowling and into the park. Turn left onto the cycle path that runs uphill behind the tennis courts.

2. At the top near the café turn left, walk across the narrow footbridge and turn right to enter the Parkland Walk.

3. The route crosses over Upper Tollington Park Road after 180 metres and then Stapleton Hall Road 400 metres later. After 245 metres it crosses over Mount Pleasant Road.

4. Pass under two close road bridges (Mount View Road and Crouch Hill, A2101) 250 metres later. There is a ramp to the right that leads to Crouch Hill Road and Crouch Hill station. Further on is a footbridge across the cutting; look up into the brick arches for a ghoulish surprise and some artistic graffiti. Pass through the deserted platforms of the former Crouch End station and under Crouch End Hill's (A103) bridge.

5. After 530 metres the track passes over Stanhope Road and Northwood Road, 300 metres later. Continue for a further 200 metres to the ramp on the left before the Holmsdale Road entrance. The trail continues for about 100 metres to the tunnel entrance, now blocked with bars and a gate.

6. Turn around and enjoy the gentle slope of the rail bed all the way back to Finsbury Park.

7. On entering the park continue straight ahead. Turn left around the barrier, joining the road which merges with the car park, so take care. The Finsbury Park Staff Yard is on your right. Keep following the road which bends around to the right; after another barrier it becomes traffic free. There is a short uphill section before a straight gentle run down to the park's main entrance. Follow the hairpin bend to the café by the lake, where the route finishes. Return to your starting point.

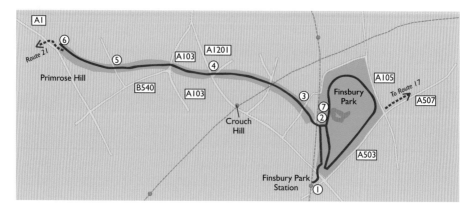

Distance: 17.4 miles. Start and finish at Tattenham Corner car park.

Map: OS Explorer maps 161 and 146, and TfL Local Cycling Guide 12.

Surface and Gradients: This route encompasses tarmac and rough roads, sealed or all-weather hard-packed paths. As horse riding is popular in this area, Bridleways are typically well drained but muddy in places when wet. This is an undulating ride with some short steep sections. It is best ridden in an anti-clockwise direction to make the most of gentler gradients.

Roads and road crossings: These quiet suburban roads have good provision for safe crossing. However, care is needed at the following points: Reigate Road (A240), Banstead High Street, Brighton Road (A217) on Banstead Downs, the Northey Avenue/Cheam Road roundabout and Cheam Road (near Ewell East station). The roads around the railway stations can be busy. If starting from Stoneleigh, take care on the short section of A24. If starting from Ewell East station, consider walking the short distance to Banstead Road.

Refreshments: Tattenham Corner has a café hut (with nearby toilets) and pub with outside seating. The Oaks Park and Nonsuch Park both have a café and toilets. There are many pubs along the route.

This is a circular ride around the North Downs east of Epsom. Initially, the route passes through Tattenham and Banstead before venturing into the countryside and Oaks Park, where the route spends a great deal of time off road on Bridleways. After crossing Banstead Downs the route returns to Cheam's sealed roads and Nonsuch Park. Returning to the downs, the route passes through Epsom.

BACKGROUND AND PLACES OF INTEREST
Epsom and Banstead Downs
Epsom Downs is the home of the Derby, the UK's premier thoroughbred horse race. It is held on open public land. Banstead Downs' chalk grassland covers 430 acres, managed by Natural England.

Warren Farm Woodland Trust Reserve
Warren Farm is owned Woodland Trust Reserve. Cyclists are allowed on its cycle ways.

Nonsuch Park
These 120 acres of rough parkland were once the site of Nonsuch Palace. Wanting a palace beyond compare (none such), Henry VIII, died before seeing it completed. The present Mansion was built in 1802-05. The 2.5 miles of cycling within the park are especially suited to children.

Starting Points & Transport:
1. Tattenham Corner station car park (2) – via Southern trains from London Bridge.
2. Oaks Park (8).
3. Ewell East station (1B) – accessible via Southern trains from Victoria.
4. Stoneleigh station (1C) – accessible via South West Trains services from Waterloo. Free parking at Tattenham Corner, Oaks Park and Alexandra Park, off the A2022 (16), and in some residential areas along the route.

Links to other routes
Route 14 – Coulsdon to Hackbridge via Mitcham Common.

ROUTE INSTRUCTIONS:
1. A) From Tattenham Corner Station: exit the station, turn right and then left, passing a garage onto Tattenham Crescent. Turn right onto Tattenham Corner Road, passing over the racecourse. Turn right up Tattenham Crescent. Go to 1 D).
   B) From Ewell station: exit the station via Platform 2 and take the footpath left up to busy Cheam Road (A232). Turn right, walking 230 metres and turning right again into quieter Banstead Road. Go to 15.
   C) From Stoneleigh station: proceed down Stoneleigh Broadway. Go straight

over the roundabout into The Glade. Turn left at the T-junction onto Chadacre. At the crossroads turn right onto Sparrow Farm Road. Turn right at the traffic lights onto busy London Road (A24) for 110 metres and then left into Nonsuch Park. Go to 14.

D) From Tattenham Corner café car park: turn left up Tattenham Crescent, passing the Tattenham Corner pub on your right. Continue uphill to a T-junction and turn left onto Great Tattenhams. Follow ⅓ mile, climbing to the Reigate Road (A240) traffic lights. Cross the junction and turn left, walking along the pavement on the opposite side for 60 metres before turning first right up Church Lane bridleway, signposted NCN 22. After ⅓ mile on gravel which changes to tarmac through the Nork Park, join residential area The Drive.

2. Cross the busy Brighton Road (A217), turn left via the second of the pedestrian crossings that feeds straight into Garretts Lane. Carry on into Court Road, which becomes Avenue Road as it bends left past the Lady Neville Recreation Ground.

3. Turn right onto busy Banstead High Street (B2217). Go right at the mini-roundabout onto Park Road and left onto Woodmansterne Lane. Less confident riders may choose to walk the 350 metres along this busy section.

4. Enter into the countryside. Pass the Woodman pub at Woodmansterne Village.

5. Turn left onto Carshalton Road, just past a small parade of shops on your right, joining a short section of Route 14 from here to Oaks Park.

6. After ¾ mile descend to the junction with Croydon Lane (A2022). Mayfield Lavender Fields are on the left. Turn left, taking the path adjacent to the road and using the Pegasus crossing to enter Oaks Park through the black metal gate.

The gardens of Nonsuch Park Mansion.

7. For the route around Oaks Park: take the road passing the tearooms (signposted NCN 20), which bends to the right. At the bottom, turn left to take the bridleway. The overlap with Route 14 ends here. After 500 metres turn left and cycle uphill to the Oaks Park. Keep left where the path steepens and forks by some steps, but take the right-hand path. The route drops down and follows around a walled garden space on your left.

8. Emerge onto the rough Fairlawn Road. Turn right and then left just before the mock Tudor House onto Freedown Lane. This is a bridleway for 300 metres before it returns to a rough road next to Highdown Prison.

9. Leave Freedown Lane to cross over Sutton Lane (A2218) to the left, onto another bridleway. This is the start of Banstead Downs.

10. Enjoy the downhill section to the bridge over the railway and keep to the left on the other side. Be alert crossing the golf course.

11. Take care crossing the very busy Brighton Road (A217). Take the bridleway to the right amongst the bushes and not the sandy track. The route runs downhill now, cutting across the golf course and through small wooded sections.

12. Return to suburbia in Sandy Lane. Take the second left onto Cuddington Way and first right onto Cheyham Way. Turn left onto Northey Avenue. Confident riders can take the right turn at the roundabout, then go uphill and left onto Bramley Road. Cautious riders can turn right onto Nonsuch Walk just before the roundabout. Walk across Cheam Road and down the steps onto the quiet Nonsuch Walk service road. Cycle uphill, turning left onto Bramley Road.

13. Cycle downhill, under the railway bridge and out onto the open grassland of Warren Farm nature reserve. Continue into the tree line and down onto The Avenue inside Nonsuch Park. Take short left/right turns to follow the tarmac path up to the mansion house. Head north away from the house along the tree-lined avenue for ½ a mile, to the park's northern boundary with London Road (A24).

14. Retrace your tracks back to the mansion but follow the path to the left of the house, onto the Fir Walk (with care near the car park.) At the T-junction turn right onto The Avenue. Turn left through Warren Farm and back out under the railway bridge, turning right onto Holmwood Road. Carry on uphill to Queensmead Road and the T-junction on Cheam Road. Turn left then first right into Banstead Road. There are cycle lane markings but it is a dangerous right turn. Consider walking from Queensmead Avenue to Banstead Road (only 120 metres).

15. After 170 metres turn right onto a shared gravel path between playing fields and a Jehovah's Witness church. The path is more or less straight ahead now for 1¼ miles crossing the following quiet residential streets: Reigate Road (A240 – toucan crossing), Ewell Downs Road, The Green, Wallace Fields, Alexandra Road (A2022 – toucan crossing), Bridle Road. Now pass through the backstreets of Epsom.

16. Turn right onto Albert Road and left onto Church Road, which curves right to become Grove Road. At the T-junction turn right onto Church Street and first left onto Worple Road. Go straight over the staggered crossing of busy Ashley Road (B290) using the mini-roundabout. After 100 metres go straight at the bend to stay on Worple Road (signposted 'leading to Chalk Lane').

17. At the T-junction turn left onto quiet Chalk Lane. Climb back up to Epsom Downs (1.1 miles).

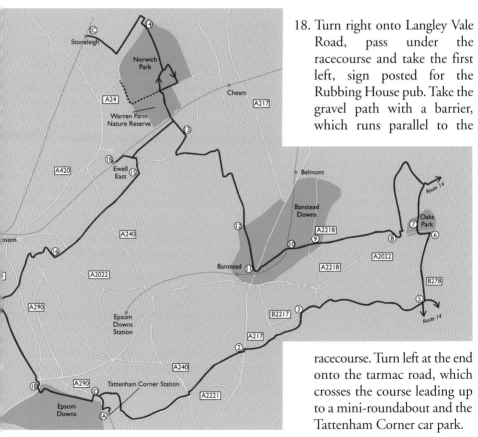

18. Turn right onto Langley Vale Road, pass under the racecourse and take the first left, sign posted for the Rubbing House pub. Take the gravel path with a barrier, which runs parallel to the racecourse. Turn left at the end onto the tarmac road, which crosses the course leading up to a mini-roundabout and the Tattenham Corner car park.

ROUTE 24
Woldingham loop

Distance: 18.6 miles if going via Warren Barn Farm up to the Croydon Road (6b). Subtract 1.5 miles if taking the very steep route through Slines Oak Wood (6a).

Map: OS Explorer maps 161 and 146. Surrey Cycle Guide No.8, or TfL Local Cycling Guide 13.

Surfaces and Gradients: A large section of the route (11.2 miles) is on quiet country roads and some hard pack or gravel tracks. The 7.5 miles of off-road paths and bridleways are well drained, but some are very muddy in places after rain. This is a hilly route that contains some very steep sections at times.

Roads and road crossings: The road downhill from Woldingham station can be busy at times. After the Warren Farm climb, care should be taken on the Croydon Road (B269), but there is an adjacent footpath for cautious cyclists. The busy Limpsfield Road (B269) is encountered twice and should be crossed with care. Take care crossing Slines New Road.

Refreshments: A friendly husband and wife team runs the Coach House pub in Chelsham, with hearty portions of good food and outside seating. There are numerous possibilities in New Addington, a short but very steep diversion from the northernmost point of the route. On the return leg the route passes the Hare and Hounds pub in Warlingham and, at the end of the ride, the Dene Coffee Shop in Woldingham.

This countryside route is still only a short train ride from the centre of London. On a clear day, the City's distinctive skyline can be seen in the distance. The route gives the rider a taste of a typical bridleway off-road ride, with a flinty well-drained path and a few muddy patches if wet. After a prolonged spell of rain it becomes very slippery, so knobbly tyres and a mountain bike are essential. Although mostly on quiet roads there are some great off-road downhills, as well as narrow paths that weave between the trees under a magnificent canopy of deciduous woods. There are some long climbs but the beauty of the countryside and its wildlife make the perfect distraction.

BACKGROUND AND PLACES OF INTEREST
Marden Park Woods
Consisting of Great Church Wood (12 acres) and Marden Park (154 acres), this is the largest site owned by the Woodland Trust in Surrey. High on the North Downs, it forms part of the Surrey Hills Area of Outstanding Natural Beauty and the Woldingham and Oxted Downs Site of Special Scientific Interest. Wildlife thrives here, including at least 25 species of butterfly, rare Roman snails, stripe-winged grasshoppers, tawny owls and roe deer. Bluebells and wood anemone flourish in spring, and bee, butterfly and common orchids may be spotted in the rich chalk grassland in early summer.

Starting Points & Transport:
Woldingham Station – accessible via southern services out of Victoria on the Oxted line. There is parking at £3.70 per day and free parking nearby at Church Road.

ROUTE INSTRUCTIONS:
1. Turn left out of the station car park, joining Church Road on the bend. Go downhill for 600 metres where the road gently sweeps left. Turn left off the road onto a gravel track signposted NCN 21. The track starts opposite a brick wall and follows the tree line uphill around a copse. Turn left onto the road. Continue straight ahead for 2.2 miles, passing Woldingham School up the valley. Keep right after the tennis courts.

2. At the barrier, turn left onto the road through the trees. After 530 metres turn sharp left up steep Gangers Hill. Look down onto the M25 motorway as the road bends left, turning right onto the bridleway to the right of the gated driveway for Hanging Wood Forest farm. The next section is a steep downhill with concrete humps across the path (to slow rainwater erosion). Take great care because the path drops down suddenly to join Tandridge Hill Lane.

3. Turn left, heading uphill for 450 metres. Turn right, rejoining Gangers Hill.

The view from the very steep Gangers Hill, with the M25 motorway in the distance.

Marden Park is opposite the junction. Turn right and then right again onto the bridleway about 100 metres from the junction. Head downhill before returning to Gangers Hill 320 metres later.

4. Head uphill and continue to the T-junction on the bend. Turn right onto The Ridge, the busiest road so far. After about 0.6 miles there is a viewpoint on the right which is worth a visit.

5. After a further 340 metres the trees thin out at the staggered crossroads. There is a high brick wall with pillars topped by spheres made of bricks. Turn left here onto Vanguard Way (signposted a dead end). Once past the houses and pylons on the right, the road heads downhill and deteriorates to a broken-up track before becoming a typical Downs bridleway that can be slimy if wet. Once clear of the trees at Greenhill Shaw, the route heads downhill towards Woldingham. Turn right onto Slines Oak Road.

6. At the bottom of the hill at Warren Barn Farm, after 560 metres the route splits:
   a) Riders who are both very fit and good climbers may wish to follow Slines Oak Road back uphill. After 330 metres turn right after the 'narrow road' sign, onto a narrow gravel path. The path steepens and is very loose. At the top of the hill, turn left onto the track that passes a house on the right. At the T-junction, cross straight over Limpsfield Road (B269) and turn right onto the shared path. Turn left onto Ledgers Road. Go to 9.
   b) To follow the longer but less demanding route, turn right onto the farm road.

7. Follow the farm road passing the Green Dragon Airsports Centre (which has a toilet!) and onto a wide gravel farm track. This is one of the longest climbs of the route.

8. At the top, cross over and turn left onto a shared footpath along the busy

Croydon Road (B269). After 650 metres turn right into Beech Farm Road Turn left after 700 metres up the gated track, towards the telephone pylons. On a clear day, Docklands and the City can be seen in the right-hand distance. The next section can be very muddy if wet and can also be churned up by horses. Keep going, crossing over the track and continuing back into the trees to turn right onto Ledgers Road.

9. Turn left off of the road at the red and white barrier across the track. Continue for about half a mile, passing Henley Wood and emerging at the crossroads with Chelsham Common Road, Church Lane and Ledgers Road. (Turn left from here to visit the Coach and Horses pub.)

10. Turn right onto Church Lane, rejoining NCN 21, and left after 400 metres, passing around a gate and onto a track through Holt Wood. Look out for horse riders. At the road junction, turn left onto Farleigh Court Road and leave NCN21. Where the road bends away to the left, turn sharp right onto a narrow path. Pass Hazelwoods Stud on the left and enter the trees. There is now a great downhill through the trees before it joins a track, passing an HGV haulage compound. Turn left onto Featherbed Lane.

11. Continue for about half a mile before turning left off the road, just after Farleigh Dean Crescent. (If a visit to the shops or restaurants of New Addington is required, turn right instead and follow the very steep tarmac path uphill. At the top turn left and then right to reach the shops across the green).

12. Climb up through Firth Wood along a flinty track with many roots. Once out of the trees, cross a golf course. The path returns uphill to a rocky tree-lined gully. Pass around the gate and cross over Farleigh Court Road into Church Road. Continue past the riding centre car park to pick up the bridleway in the opposite corner. Look out for horses. The bridleway eventually emerges from the woods and joins Daniels Lane.

13. Cross over Harrow Road and go up the broken tarmac track; after the sports ground on the right this gives way to a bumpy unsealed track.

14. Join Farleigh Road on a bend and turn left to go downhill. This road can be busy at

Sign for NCN 21 off the Chelsham Common Road.

times of the day, so cautious riders can take the pavement on the opposite side. Go straight at the mini-roundabout onto Sunny Bank and take the first left (after the speed hump) onto Green Hill Lane. Keep going straight on as it runs into a typical Downs bridleway.

15. Turn left onto Chelsham Common Road. There is pavement here for cautious riders. Continue uphill for 500 metres. Turn right onto the bridleway, signposted 'Gatwick and Waldingham' on NCN 21.(If refreshments are needed continue straight ahead on Chelsham Common Road, taking the first left for the Coach House pub). Pass through the woods with the cemetery on the right, then join Rogers Lane before crossing busy Limpsfield Road [B269] onto High Lane. The Hare and Hounds pub and a superstore are up Limpsfield Road on the right.)

16. The narrow tarmac road bends around to the left, passing houses amidst the trees. The route turns right down Plantation Lane, which becomes a bridleway and runs downhill with views of the golf course on the left. The surface has been covered with wood bark chippings to improve the wet weather conditions. At the bottom, turn left onto the golf course road and pass the clubhouse. Just before the pillared entrance, pick up the bridleway on the right. After 330 metres turn left to cross Halliloo Valley Road (formerly Slines New Road) on a bend. This is a very dangerous crossing, so listen out for traffic speeding up the hill and around the bend. Follow the NCN 21 signs down to Church Road and the point where the route turned off the road for the very first time. Turn left to cycle uphill to Woldingham station. Cautious cyclists can use the pavement. Look out for cars coming out of the large garden centre.

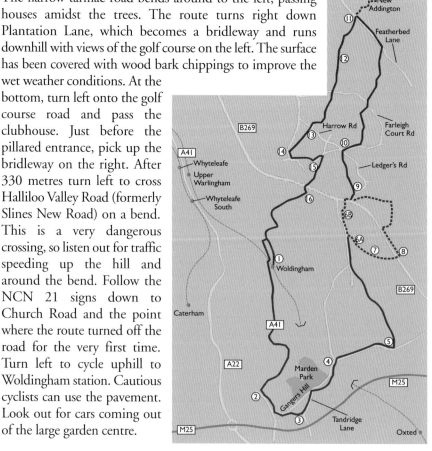

Distance: 13.7 miles, but this can easily be shortened or lengthened on paths.
Map: OS Explorer map 174. There is also a map inside a cycling pamphlet available from the visitors centre at High Beach or the City of London website.
Surface and Gradients: Hard-packed gravel paths which can be used all year around. Smaller paths throughout the forest. Most are fine in dry conditions but muddy when wet or strewn with roots. The forest has many short steep inclines.
Roads and road crossings: Apart from the short section near Chingford station the route is traffic-free, although crosses roads. The A104 is particularly busy.
Refreshments: Numerous refreshment facilities in and around Epping Forest. To the south of Queen Elizabeth's Hunting Lodge is Butler's Retreat, a kiosk café. Chingford offers more choices. There is a kiosk in the car park on the corner of Fairmead Road and Cross Roads, a short distance from the Robin Hood pub. At High Beach is another kiosk, as well as the King's Oak pub. The Old Orleans Restaurant is at the Wake Arms Roundabout (A104 and A121). There are two pubs (Forester's Arms and Gardener's Arms) at Baldwins Hill, near Baldwins Pond. The Visitors Centre at High Beach has toilets. There is a public toilet and water fountain in the stable block by Queen Elizabeth's Hunting Lodge.

Epping Forest is a mountain biker's heaven! This route is intended as an introduction to familiarise the reader, inviting them to venture 'off-piste' and really have some fun. Apart from the two ancient earthworks and Loughton Brook's ecological reserve, cyclists have free reign. A Global Positioning System (GPS) is very useful, but a compass is more reliable in the denser parts of the forest. The main paths are wide, all-weather and traffic free, and so would be suitable for children's first off-road ride. However, there are road crossings to be made, so take care.

BACKGROUND AND PLACES OF INTEREST

Epping Forest

The forest stretches for 12 miles, from east London to southwest Essex, and at nearly 6000 acres is the largest of a number of open spaces owned and managed by the Corporation of London. It is a haven for walkers, horse riders, anglers and cyclists with its ancient woodland, grassy plains, heathland, rivers, ponds and lakes. As well as being an important recreational centre and wildlife habitat, two thirds of it is designated a Site of Special Scientific Interest and a Special Area of Conservation. There are thousands of magnificent ancient oak, beech and hornbeam trees, and meadows rich with wild flowers, skylarks, butterflies and dragonflies, wildfowl and fallow deer. This is a former royal hunting forest. History enthusiasts will enjoy Queen Elizabeth's Hunting Lodge at Chingford.

Ambresbury Banks

Site of the remains of an Iron Age hill fort. Finds at the site suggest a construction date of around 700BC and occupation until 42AD. It is surrounded by a 2-metre bank together with a ditch, which encircle an area of 11 acres. The area is now completely wooded but would have been cleared of trees to enable a better field of view.

Starting Points and Parking:

1. Chingford station – accessible via National Express East Anglia train services on the Lee Valley line from Liverpool Street.
2. Bury Road car park.

There are free car parks all over Epping Forest.

0

Route 17 – The River Lea Navigation, 2.3 miles to the west.

ROUTE INSTRUCTIONS:

1. Exit Chingford station, walk over the zebra crossing to turn right and cycle along Station Road. Take the second left into Bury Road and the first track on the right to enter Chingford Plain. This is only 260 metres from the station and so could easily be walked.

2. Keep going straight ahead until six footpaths meet at a crossroads. Turn left over the stream and head parallel with the car park towards the forest.

3. A) Younger or inexperienced mountain bikers may wish to turn right onto the wide path and cycle along the edge of the forest. The path enters

Looking along the Ambresbury Banks.

the trees for a while before turning left onto Green Ride, a rusty-coloured track. B) More adventurous riders can continue into the forest on a narrow single-track path that meanders through the trees. After about 400 metres, cross the wide path back into the forest and onto the narrower path. Keep going ahead or right through the next section to finally join Green Ride. Turn left.

4. There is a break in the trees as a path joins from the left. Keep going straight ahead. The main track bends to the right, cutting a corridor between the trees, but go straight onto the wide sandy track. It bends to the right, opening out into a grassy area, before bending right again at a complicated junction of paths.

5. Go straight ahead over the apex of the bend, crossing the grassy area for the car park. Don't get drawn to the right on the main track or any smaller tracks.

6. To the north of the car park, follow the horse ride to the left of the livestock holding pen. Follow the bridleway north uphill. After about 500 metres, take one of the minor paths to the right to visit the snack kiosk on the corner of Cross Roads and Fairmead Road. Otherwise, continue ahead until emerging at Cross Roads. Cross diagonally to the right to enter the gated sandy track. This section has a wonderful succession of steep ups and downs.

7. Turn sharp left down Nursery Road to visit the Epping Forest Visitors Centre or King's Oak pub; cross straight over the road to continue. Take care at the bend in the road, as dense vegetation restricts the view. Turn left for the snack kiosk in the car park or right to take the gated track on the left. Follow the track up to the road.

8. Cross over Claypit Lane.
   A) Those who enjoy downhilling and have the stamina for the climb back up should turn left off the major track after the metal gate. Follow as straight ahead as possible. The path plummets down the hillside; local riders have made tabletop jumps and ramps on the way down. Once at the bottom, you can choose to return up Claypit Lane or cross over into Pynest Green Lane and take the first path on the left. Keep going uphill, curving slightly to the left to emerge back into the car park. Return to Claypit Lane.
   B) Keep going straight on the wide track.

9. Cross over the busy Woodridden Hill (A121) back onto the track and follow it to the right, almost back to the road. Turn left behind the Old Orleans Restaurant. The path crosses a minor road before running parallel to the busy High Road (B1393).

10. Cross with care and continue along the main sandy track up to a T-junction. Turn left and stay on track for 1.1 miles until, at the top of the hill, the trees open out and the track bends to the right. A smaller track leads off to the left and another runs straight on, forming a small grassy triangle.

11. Carry straight on through the trees onto an open piece of ground where the M25 is directly below! Return through the trees, turning right onto the path. Pass the pond and follow the path which swings over close to the road, to avoid the Ambresbury Banks. Don't be tempted to ride on them because it could damage this unique archaeological feature. The path finally leads back onto the sandy track first ridden after crossing the B1393. Turn left, going up to the T-junction to turn right.

12. Continue past a car park and cross Coppice Row (B172) and another little car park (Jack's Hill) before the track starts to undulate its way south for 0.8 miles.

13. Pass to the left of the car park and cross the busy A121 again. The wide track sweeps left and right throughout the next section.

14. After 0.8 miles the first of two wide paths crosses the track. Carry straight on.

The Green Ride is a typical rusty hard-packed gravel track found throughout Epping Forest.

15. Cross Earl's Path after a further 0.75 miles. Pass to the left of a pond. After 150 metres leave the light coloured track, turning right to pass a bigger pond on the left. The path then becomes a typical forest track through the trees.

16. Emerge from the trees at a car park. Cross with care over busy Epping New Road (A104) and go through a wooden gate to a sandy track across open ground. Cross Fairmead Road and go back into the trees where the wide track bends to the left. Keep going for 750 metres until the huge oak tree and a crossroad of paths.

17. Swing left off the main track to emerge from the trees. Turn right onto the end of Fairmead Road and go around the metal gate. Don't take the first obvious sandy footpath on the right. Take the rough bridle path about 10 metres further on the right to emerge onto the busy Ranger's Road (A1069).

18. Continue on the bridleway opposite until reaching the open grassy area. The Warren Wood pub is directly ahead through the trees. Turn right down the grassy area and left onto the sandy path away from the road. Follow it over a stream and into the trees. Emerge onto an open area and take the first right over the bridge. Return to the trees on a wide sandy track. Pass to the right of Warren Pond on the gravel road to cross Ranger's Road again.

19. Directly opposite is Queen Elizabeth's Hunting Lodge. To the right is Butler's Retreat café. Follow the path around the back of Butler's Retreat and head for the car park to end the ride back at Chingford.

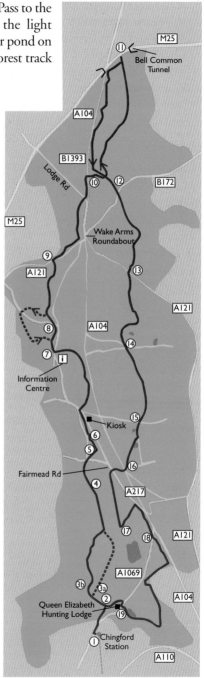

INDEX